MAN
DOWN

MAN
DOWN

DAN ABRAMS

Proof Beyond a Reasonable Doubt

That Women Are Better

Cops, Drivers, Gamblers, Spies,

World Leaders, Beer Tasters, Hedge Fund

Managers, and Just About Everything Else

ABRAMS IMAGE, NEW YORK

Editor: Jennifer Levesque
Designer: Laura Klynstra
Production Manager: Tina Cameron

Cataloging-in-Publication Data has been applied for and may be obtained from the Library of Congress.
ISBN 978-0-8109-9829-2

Printed and bound in U.S.A.
10 9 8 7 6 5 4 3 2 1

Abrams Image books are available at special discounts when purchased in quantity for premiums and
promotions as well as fundraising or educational use. Special editions can also be created to specification.
For details, contact specialmarkets@abramsbooks.com or the address below.

ABRAMS
THE ART OF BOOKS SINCE 1949
115 West 18th Street
New York, NY 10011
www.abramsbooks.com

CONTENTS

PREFACE

Why is Dan Abrams, the legal guy from TV, writing a book about women? As I worked on this book, I was repeatedly asked that entirely fair question. After all, my career has been primarily devoted to constitutional debates, salacious legal tales, media analysis, web entrepreneurship, and corporate management. What in that experience possibly qualifies me to weigh in on a battle of the sexes? I'm not going to bore you with some hackneyed claim about the importance of the women in my life (which is not to minimize that reality). Nor am I presuming to possess rare insight into women. Let me be clear: I don't. In many ways I remain as bewildered by women as when I was a single man in my midtwenties. Today, as a, well, still single guy in my midforties, I can offer no valuable guidance to men or relationship advice to women for that matter. I remain a consumer of such information, not an expert.

This book is far simpler than that. I am a lawyer, and I have found the evidence of female superiority to be beyond compelling.

It started when I read a lighthearted article about how women are better than men in various professions. Some of these surprised me, so I researched a little to see which ones were actually backed up by legitimate studies. A few were; others were not (one of the areas, for example, was law, but I did not find the evidence either compelling or entertaining enough to make it into this book). In the process, however, I found more and then yet more studies—evidence—that reached the same conclusion.

Early on, I developed a thesis consistent with a sentiment I have long believed to be true: women, as a group, are more deliberative, compassionate, and thoughtful than men. So I assumed that most of the examples I found would relate to intellect, health, communication, and interpersonal skills. Some did, but I quickly found empirical evidence that women are also the superior gender in many other, less obvious areas. Simple research uncovered scores of underreported or nearly ignored studies and research that seem to demonstrate that mano a womano, the womanos come out on top.

So as any lawyer might, I have taken the evidence and condensed it into what I hope is a cogent "argument" of sorts. But for a lawyer, bringing the right case is only part of the equation. *When* you bring that case can be crucial as well. So why now? Because the vast majority of the studies referenced here come from the past few years. This is hardly surprising, since only in the past two decades or so have women finally been afforded similar professional and even social opportunities. The obvious consequence is that only now can we evaluate on a fairly level playing field how the girls stack up against the boys.

And why should a member of the losing team chronicle the victory? Well, I guess you could argue it adds credibility to have someone with no vested interest in winning do the job. Lawyers are chosen that way all the time.

But I had the help of a winning team. First, I want to thank my amazing research assistant and collaborator, Frances Martel.

Frances began by doing research for me, but by the end she felt more like a partner in this project. With her wit, humor, and smarts, she helped make it what it is. After all, how could I write a book about women being better than men without a woman's touch? I also want to thank James Camp for his excellent early work on the project, Sarah Devlin for helping me make my deadlines, and of course my mother, Efrat; my sister, Ronnie; and my nieces, Dylan, Teddy, and Finn, for reminding me every day why this all matters.

OPENING
STATEMENT

You are about to take a guided tour of an array of studies and polls that make the case, as it has not been made before, for women. At the conclusion of this book, when you have seen and digested all the evidence, I believe you will have to agree that the evidence is overwhelming.

But before we embark on this journey, let me begin in reverse with what this case for women is *not*. It is not a celebration of history's great women. Scores of spectacular women have changed the world for the better. From political leaders to entertainers, from advocates for social change to writers, women have made decisions, taken risks, and advanced society in ways that should be and have been recognized and publicly celebrated. That, however, is not the object here.

Nor is this a mere exercise in reverse sexism. Men aren't uniformly inferior to women. They test better in certain subjects and tend to be stronger, taller, and faster than women. I am not convinced that women, as a group, play basketball or read maps (see Chapter 20) better than men.

The evidence here will show, however, that women are living longer and evolving better. They are shining brighter on intelligence tests and displaying a larger appetite at eating competitions. Data suggest that women are more effective gamblers, savvier spies, and more successful hedge fund managers. As leaders, in our marketplace as well as our capitals, men may outnumber women—but they are also outperformed by them. And when the going gets rough, you may want to seek out a female doctor, cop, or even loan officer.

There are inevitably going to be holes in the argument, and obviously every woman isn't better than every man. (I mean, those damn male drivers do get annoying on the road when you need to be somewhere in a hurry, but that doesn't mean *all* women are better drivers.) That said, this book isn't just the expression of an opinion; it's evidence. In nearly every field, statistics and studies show that women are better collaborators, are more cautious, and are more adept at navigating treacherous terrain. In nearly every field, their error rate is lower. And since women also endure pain better than men, the sting of learning of their inferiority may be tough on the guys.

I think the research will show that a somewhat sexist cliché about men and women is misleading. Behind every great man, there is a great woman? A truer truism would be that behind every great man there is probably an even greater woman—and in most cases, she ought to be out in front.

In sum, when you examine all the evidence presented here, as you might during a trial, I think you can come to only one conclusion: that there is proof beyond a reasonable doubt that women are better than men.

PART I

WOMEN ARE COOLER

CHAPTER 1

Women Handle Failed Relationships Better

Is there a cure for a broken heart?
Only time can heal your broken heart,
just as time can heal his
broken arms and legs.
—MISS PIGGY

These days, there are probably few film genres quite as commercial-ized and dependent on stereotypes as the "chick flick." Its cornerstone is the stereotype of women as the more emotional and often weaker and needier gender. The plots so infrequently vary that it usually takes about fifteen minutes to figure out the entire story (and conclu-sion): A gorgeous female protagonist navigates the impossibly rocky dating scene of some metropolis so big she fails to see true love right before her eyes as she pines for a callous playboy over her own chick flick and a bucket of ice cream. Inevitably, she makes the right choice and abandons her grief over the playboy in exchange for a fairy-tale ending with the nice guy who waited for her to get over her ex.

They're movies seemingly designed for a heartbroken girl to devour empty calories over while she tries to forget her loser ex-boyfriend. Women need these films (the movie industry hopes) because it must take several months of romantic comedies and maxed-out credit cards before the wounded girls feel comfortable proceeding to the next relationship—this as the men are supposedly out and about hours later, happily meeting scores of other "chicks."

Unfortunately for the reputation of "emotionally bulletproof" men worldwide, the research shows just the opposite—it's actually men who should be buying discounted boxes of Kleenex with the club card after a breakup.

Sociologists at Wake Forest University and Florida State University released a study in June 2010 that showed women are affected less by bad relationships and handle failed relationships better. One thousand unmarried young men and women were asked a variety of questions on relationships, and their answers showed that women and men deal with breakups differently—women become more depressed, men turn more to substance abuse—but on the whole, women are better able to deal with the stress of failed relationships.

Why? The study's authors found that young men tended to turn to friends and family for support less than women did, making it more difficult to cope with the feelings of loneliness that come with separation. (There was no word on whether they also resorted to food and romantic comedies at lower rates, but I'm not sure that most brokenhearted men are going to rush out and rent *Love Actually* after being dumped.)

To make matters worse, males more than females tend to receive a greater portion of their emotional support from their significant others. Women, meanwhile, tend to rely on their other social ties after breakups, making the transition to single life smoother.

So it's not exactly that men are more sensitive to a breakup; it's that they have a harder time getting the necessary support to get through it. In covering the study, the UK *Telegraph* quoted a sociologist at University College London, who explained: "Young men don't tend to confide in each other and that can make them feel isolated. Their friendship groups are more competitive than nurturing. They are just as sensitive as women but it's a matter of whether they feel valued."

This may be news to some, but not to observant Jews who have suspected it for centuries. In fact, Jewish mourning traditions designate a significantly longer period of mourning for widowers than for widows when dealing with the most traumatic and permanent breakups of all: death. Men may have to wait for as long as a year before marrying again. Well-known Rabbi Maurice Lamm wrote on Chabad.org that "evidently, the wife was considered better able to control her emotions." The longer mourning period for male Jews is an effort to "temper his despair, [so] he would not enter a second marriage with the first love still fresh in mind."

So no, a woman's heart isn't any more fragile than a man's; she's just more likely to shield it with the right armor. Faced with the exact same problem, women tend to openly choose the more effective solution—friends, family, and the willingness to cry on shoulders—over sucking it up and trying to convince everyone that they're "cool with it."

CHAPTER 2

Women Tolerate Pain Better (and Men Bitch About It More)

Beauty is pain. It IS painful.
But we women are tough—we have
babies and all kinds of stuff.
—BEAUTICIAN/BODY WAXER LISA SMITH

The movie *The 40-Year-Old Virgin* has numerous memorable and hilarious lines surrounding the absurd life of Steve Carell as Andy Stitzer, a sweet, naive electronics store employee who has somehow never quite gotten around to having sex. But there is one particular scene that is as painful as it is hilarious, at least for the guys to watch. It occurs after Andy's friends convince him that he needs to wax his unusually thick mane of chest hair. To make it that much more authentic, the scene is played out in real life, with Carell having chunks of his man patch yanked out with hot wax on camera, followed by understandably loud yelps. While his chest (and nipple) hair was particularly dense, waxing is a chore many more women endure than men, and most of the time they don't complain, much less yell and scream.

We generally don't tend to think of pain as pink and flowery. Women are meant to heal the wounds, not fight through them, right? Well, as it turns out, the Carrie Bradshaws may actually be able to "take it like a man" better than the Andy Stitzers or even Rambos.

For starters, women actually experience more pain than men throughout their lifetimes, and not just because of waxing or even childbirth. According to psychologist Dr. Ed Keogh, researchers at the University of Bath found that "women experience a greater number of pain episodes across their life span than men, in more bodily areas and with greater frequency."

Why? Many explanations have been presented but one of them comes from the medical journal *Plastic and Reconstructive Surgery*, which states, "On average, women have 34 nerve fibers per square centimeter of facial skin. Men average just 17," making any facial sensations more pronounced for women. Another possible explanation? Men's brains have a "pain-suppressing circuit" that in women is wired differently, and less effectively, according to a 2008 report from the University of Georgia in Athens (cited in *New Scientist*).

Now scientists are starting to believe Nietzsche's aphorism "That which does not kill me makes me stronger." A series of studies conducted in 2003 showed that not only was there evidence of estrogen being a major factor in suppressing pain, but, according to Columbia University Professor James Dillard, as quoted by redOrbit.com, "Research has shown that the more upset somebody is about pain ... the more they tend to amplify pain signals and the worse the pain feels. So, if a woman is used to pain, she will be less alarmed by pain signals, and that leads to better tolerance."

Where better to prove that than by examining the numbers from a job that includes enduring pain: the military. A study of vets reported by the *New York Times* in October 2009 showed that among soldiers using the Veterans Affairs health system, women were less likely to report pain:

> In a review of the records of veterans of the wars in Iraq or Afghanistan, researchers at the Yale University School of Medicine and Veterans Affairs Connecticut Health Care System found that women were less likely than men to report any pain, 38.1 percent to 44 percent.
>
> By a smaller margin, 18 percent to 21.2 percent, the women veterans were also less likely than the men to report having persistent pain.

Of course, evaluating pain in soldiers is complicated by the differing types of injuries suffered, so how about a much simpler example: guys whining about the sniffles. A 2010 study by the UK group Engage Mutual questioned men and women about their partners' behavior when ill. Women reported that more than half of the men with the common cold will exaggerate, referring to it as a "flu" and calling the accompanying headache a "migraine." In comparison, only 40 percent of men reported that their female partners exaggerated their symptoms when they were ill. All this, despite the fact that on average men suffer fewer bouts of sickness per year than their female counterparts. (The study also found that women tend to be more sympathetic to a man with a cold than vice versa. Oy, *that* is a whole other debate.)

For those who find real studies and research tiresome, I invite you to check out the be-all and end-all of urban legends, Discovery Channel's *MythBusters*. The *MythBusters* crew carried out a simple controlled pain experiment—dunking warm hands into ice-cold buckets of water—and split their results by gender. Subjects were requested to keep their hands in the water for three minutes or until they were no longer able to tolerate the pain. The men averaged 84.3 seconds with their hands in the tank. The women? 100.4 seconds, almost 20 percent longer than the time the men were able to stand it. And if *MythBusters* says it, it's so!

The bottom line: in a variety of situations—immediate and long-term, controlled and uncontrolled—women prove capable of handling more pain than their male counterparts, despite having been dealt the bad hand of having to experience more pain on average across their lifetimes. So while the boys cover their eyes thinking of the pain poor Andy Stitzer had to endure, many women are probably just thinking, *Whatever, been there, done that.*

CHAPTER 3

Women Are Better Beer (and Wine) Tasters

*Give me a woman who loves beer
and I will conquer the world.*

—KAISER WILHELM II

One of the most effective ad campaigns of all time was one that transcended a brand. A beer company wanted to try to convince men that drinking a new lighter beer was not for weight-conscious "girls" but, rather, for big, tough guys. The seemingly ubiquitous Miller Lite beer advertisements of the early eighties were designed to reassure men that they did not lose any degree of virility by drinking a lower-calorie brew. Big, tough football players bickered over whether it just "tasted great" or was "less filling."

Ah, if they had only known that the girls could probably better answer that question, at least whether it tastes great (who knows, maybe the men can better assess how a six-pack of brew makes their butts look in clothes). Yes, brewers around the world are finding that women are more sensitive to the flavors in beer and are, therefore, better beer tasters. The *Wall Street Journal* reported that SABMiller, which makes Miller, Coors, Grolsch, and Peroni, among others, found "empirical evidence" demonstrating that women are better at detecting the chemicals that make beer go bad or "skunky."

Beer tasting is serious business for these multinational companies, and these sampling gigs have long included about as many women as a game of quarters at a frat house. But the *Journal* reported that after SABMiller decided to dig into its own employee pool to find the top tasters, they emerged with many of the female secretaries and marketers at the top of the tasting pool. The article also noted that Carlsberg, of Denmark, reported women outperforming men in a test of its tasters.

Why? Not because they're drinking more of it. Seventy-three percent of beer sales around the world are still made to guys (and I'm not sure that drinking more is exactly a talent or badge of honor either). As discussed in Chapter 28, women just have a better sense of smell, which immediately offers them an advantage over the guys in isolating flavors and scents.

Taste comes from both the sense of smell and the number of taste buds (papillae) on the tongue. Women already have half an advantage on the smell side, but it also turns out they are more likely to have a greater number of more-sensitive taste buds than men. According to University of Florida scholar Linda Bartoshuk, who conducted research into gender differences and taste for most of the nineties, this translates into many more women having "supertaster" capabilities—the ability to sense the ever so subtle differences. Thirty-five percent of all women fit this category as compared to just 15 percent of men, Bartoshuk said in an interview with PBS.

And that's not just a beer thing either; it serves women well in analyzing another alcoholic beverage—namely wine. While the world of wine tasting has tended to open its doors hesitantly to women, it's tough to forever exclude the gender with the biological advantage.

In ancient times, Greeks and Egyptians looked down upon women who even drank wine. They believed that in comparison to men, women became disproportionately wanton and reckless after drinking (this may have been a result of the fact that men diluted their wine with water and women did not). In our time, it only took eight hundred years for the Jurade of Saint-Émilion—the most prestigious Bordeaux brotherhood—to admit women, in the year 2000. And it wasn't just a change of heart on sexism that changed their minds. No, in the end they realized it was good for business.

Of course this means that taste competitions are increasingly becoming a woman's game. SABMiller's relatively new annual "taster of the year" competition—where panelists compete in blind tastings identifying beer types, smells, and chemicals—has been monopolized by Joanna Wasilewska, a former secretary at a brewery in Poland who won both of the first two events.

According to that *Wall Street Journal* article, Joanna now runs tasting panels: "She says she doesn't know why she is so good at it but thinks it may have something to do with her long love affair with perfumes. 'As a young girl I tried to learn every single perfume by heart,' she says, 'I never dreamed that I might use my skills.'" I can just picture future beer-tasting training sessions including burly guys being tested on whether those hints of melon, cedar, and citrus are from Chanel No. 5 or Estée Lauder Pleasures.

CHAPTER 4

Women Are Better Spies

*Every man is surrounded by a
neighborhood of voluntary spies.*

—JANE AUSTEN

The entertainment industry loves nothing more than a hot female spy. Think Angelina Jolie as Evelyn Salt, Jennifer Garner as CIA agent Sydney Bristow in the television show *Alias*, Julia Roberts as Claire Stenwick in *Duplicity*, Charlize Theron as the title character in *Aeon Flux*. Watching beautiful women dupe men with their charm, high-powered weapons, and wily ways appears to be an on-screen recipe for success.

Speaking of recipes, in real life, many were stunned to learn that the recipe queen, beloved American chef Julia Child, was a spy for the American Office of Strategic Services (OSS) during World War II and one of the more successful ones at that. Before she began stuffing French ducks, Julia Child helped target German submarines.

Unfortunately, it is nearly impossible for any academic or social scientist to gain access to the kind of information required for a scientifically rigorous study on espionage quality, gender-specific or otherwise: not providing information is the name of the game. Important factors like the quantity of information collected per agent, time spent out on a mission, or the identities of the agents themselves are rarely accessible. We can, however, rely on informal information-gathering experiments and the testimony of those on the inside of major intelligence operations. It appears that much of what often makes being a woman in a man's world that much harder also allows women access to information that men would be less likely to share with their brethren.

Maxwell Knight was one of the most successful members of the UK's MI5 intelligence operation. He served as a secret spy runner for MI5 while keeping his day job as a radio and television personality in the 1950s—and even got his own Bond character out of the deal. In a secret 1945 memo, reported by the *Guardian* in 2004, Knight detailed why he preferred female agents to males. Knight warned against "a great deal of nonsense" claiming that men were the superior spies. He argued the opposite:

> [I]n the history of espionage and counter-espionage a very high percentage of the greatest coups have been brought off by women. . . . It is frequently alleged that women are less discreet than men; that they are ruled by their emotions and not by their brains: that they rely on intuition rather than on reason. . . . My very own experience has been very much to the contrary. During the present war, MS [Knight's section of MI5] has investigated probably hundreds of

cases of loose talk; in by far the greater proportion . . . the offenders were men.

In other words, men will more willingly spill the beans (I guess in Julia Child's case, secret beans) to a woman than to one of his male buddies. And for intelligence gathering that means male intelligence agents are more likely to leak and male informants are more likely to talk to females.

The CIA has been significantly more mum in touting the achievements of its women, though its precursor, the OSS, was known for its stellar female agents. CIA Executive Director Nora Slatkin said in a speech to the Chicago Council of Foreign Relations in 1996 that the OSS "hired thousands of women to work in many types of jobs," and while "we may never know the true extent of the accomplishments of the women of OSS," those on the inside report that female stereotypes were way off the mark.

Regardless, anecdotes from a few intelligence workers who have discussed some of the fascinating classified details their agencies seek to hide are just that: anecdotal. What if a researcher could send out intelligence gatherers and monitor their progress as it happens? Thomas Ryan of Provide Security did precisely that in July 2010 . . . sort of. The *Washington Times* reported that Ryan, using a false, attractive female identity, set out to connect with as many government intelligence employees as he could, through online tools such as Facebook, Twitter, and LinkedIn. Ryan told the website Computerworld.com that he found it shockingly easy to connect with male professionals and to gather information like e-mails, bank accounts, and business relationships. He noted that

82 percent of men responded positively to friend requests, compared with 18 percent of women. Ryan concluded that the ease with which he managed to collect information was directly related to the fact that the alias and picture he used was "an *attractive* girl" (I guess that explains all the spam Twitter accounts with pictures of beautiful women). "It definitely had to do with looks," he said, and predicted confidently that if he had used an attractive male figure, he would have been far less successful.

Ryan's theory is backed up by science as well. A 2009 study by Radboud University in the Netherlands found that—shocker—male brains become impaired in the presence of beautiful women, no matter how intelligent the man may be. According to the *Telegraph*, which reported the research, "Men who spend even a few minutes in the company of an attractive woman perform less well in tests designed to measure brain function than those who chat to someone they do not find attractive." Meanwhile, the women didn't even flinch at the presence of an attractive male. So the presence of attractive women effectively renders a significant portion of men about as useful as slightly drunken sailors, while women remain stone-cold sober.

And it's not just the professionals who have mastered the art of information gathering—the amateur female spy is significantly more proficient than the curious male too. A May 2010 study on spousal behavior found that females were significantly more successful in collecting information on their mates. The trick? They were far more likely to go a step further than sniffing sports jackets for unfamiliar perfume. According to a survey by the London School of Economics and Nottingham Trent University (reported on by the tech blog Blorge), 14 percent of wives read their husbands' e-mail, 13 percent read text messages, and 10 percent go as far as to check their husbands' browser histories for dating websites or other unseemly corners of the internet. The men? Only about 8 percent check their wives' e-mails, and 7 percent look at texts and browser histories. Sure, it's possible that women are simply more suspicious than men (who are probably convinced that a woman is "too into him" to do anything untoward—see Chapter 13). You can also argue that they're just bigger snoops, but then again, what is a spy other than a professional snoop?

Taken as a whole, there is ample evidence to suggest that women—from your mother to a top-level female CIA operative to your favorite French chef—are master undercover operatives, and not just because men want to see them on screen either. Let's just hope our enemies don't catch on.

CHAPTER 5

Women Are Better Competitive Eaters

You can't know what a woman is like until you see her at her food.

—NERO WOLFE IN *KILL NOW—PAY LATER* (1961)

It's fairly common lore that women are masters in the kitchen. In fact, it's a kind of positive stereotype that has been distorted into something negative; the kitchen is the place misogynists like to send girls when they step out of line. But the eating part, or in particular the gorging oneself part, has long been considered a more male endeavor. So in the realm of competitive eating—yes, it's a sport—is one where assumptions dictate few women would dare enter. There's just something unladylike about stuffing your face ravenously with hot dogs, cannolis, asparagus—what have you.

And then there's the culture surrounding the sport—anyone who has ever tuned in to ESPN on the Fourth of July will know that the difference between a major World Wrestling Entertainment event and the world-renowned Nathan's Famous Hot Dog Eating Contest is only somewhat evident. The latter is a noisy, messy, haughty display of machismo, funny hats, and gastrointestinal superiority. And if the eating isn't manly enough, the sideshows—most notably, the 2010 arrest of former champion Takeru Kobayashi for disturbing the peace after titleholder Joey Chestnut taunted that he wasn't a "real man"—make it clear that the world of competitive eating is a man's world.

Or at least it tries to be. But sadly, even in this grossest of athletic-ish challenges, men have a hard time keeping up. Despite the popularity of larger-than-life characters like Chestnut and Kobayashi, it's been a 100-pound Korean American woman who has regularly put them to shame. Sonya Thomas is the most successful female competitive eater in history, currently holding more than twenty records according to the International Federation of Competitive Eating. Among her most prestigious titles are Armour Vienna Sausage, Baked Beans (Long Course), Buffalo Chicken Tenders, Catfish, Cheesecake, Chicken Nuggets, Turducken (that's a turkey stuffed with a duck stuffed with a chicken), Toasted Ravioli, Tacos, Sweet Potato Casserole, Quesadillas, Oysters, Oysters (Short Form), Meatballs, Mince Pies, Jambalaya, Hamburgers, Fruitcake, and Eggs, and the list goes on.

What exactly does a record in any of these categories look like? Well, she can eat sixty-five eggs in six minutes, eighty chicken nuggets in five. The heavier food, rather than being measured by the item, is measured in pounds. Thomas can eat ten pounds and three ounces of meatballs in ten minutes, and eleven pounds of cheesecake in nine minutes.

Sure, Thomas has been unable to overpower greats like Kobayashi and Chestnut at some of the most prestigious eating tournaments in America, including the Nathan's Famous, but in the all-around tournaments, requiring the most versatile speed and consumption skills, it's the girls who often come out on top. These are the eating equivalent of the ever-prestigious Olympic decathlon as opposed to just the sprint. On this one, it isn't Thomas, but Juliet Lee, who, at Thomas's weight class, holds the Cranberry Sauce title as well as the Ultimate Eating Tournament crown. For that, she ate seven chicken wings, a pound of nachos, three hot dogs, two "personal pizzas," and three Italian ices in seven minutes and thirteen seconds. Talk about versatility.

So what is it, exactly, that could give women the edge? It may be that they are more efficient and methodical. It also might be that they better monitor their opponents' progress to gain a competitive advantage. According to studies conducted on what could be called the opposite of competitive eating—eating disorders—women are shockingly adept at measuring the food intake of the people around them. Studies from the University of Toronto at Mississauga found that when women go out to eat together, they tend to gauge their food intake by the people around them. The study's leader, Professor Patricia Pliner, wrote in the *International Journal of Eating Disorders*, "Women are amazingly accurate at knowing how much other women around them eat." Knowing how the competitors are doing at any given time of a race is essential to pacing yourself (which women do better in long-distance running: see Chapter 22; this is no different in competitive eating).

Skeptics may argue that women don't hold the top hot dog eating title and there are far more male competitors with top rankings. First of all, Sonya Thomas holds more titles than Chestnut, and that is made even more amazing when one considers how unappealing the "sport" has been for women. Culturally, women in the West are considered "more feminine, more concerned about appearance, better looking, than larger eaters"—this according to a different study from 2008 by Professor Pliner's team. So the fact that there are even two top female competitive eaters in America and that one of them holds the overall title and the other holds another thirty-three goes to show the potential that could be unleashed if women become more comfortable with the idea of competitive eating. But with more than two women competing and winning tournaments, Joey Chestnut is going to have to do more than challenge manhood to get his female competitors arrested for disturbing the peace.

CHAPTER 6

Women Are Better with Hammers

These women just need a man in the house. That's all they need. Most of the feminists need a man to tell them what time of day it is and to lead them home.

—JERRY FALWELL

When one thinks of the prototypical gift for the "man in your life," a multifaceted toolbox (preferably filled with power tools) often lands near the top of the list. Regardless of whether the guy has turned his garage into a massive repair shed where he also carves original woodwork and rebuilds engines or is just a city boy who occasionally screws in a lightbulb, most guys just can't seem to resist the allure of the all-in-one tool kit. (Maybe there's just something about Bob Vila's plaid work shirts that gets them.) And then there are the actual tools: those different sizes and shapes of screwdrivers, pliers, and, of course, hammers serve as a sort of male catnip.

Hammers in particular may conjure up visions of guys toiling away on the new roof or garage door and then gloating about the injuries to their hands from whatever complex repair project they just completed. That gloating is not unfounded; it turns out guys may not only be bragging about those injuries more, they are also probably *getting injured* more than women as well. According to a 2009 study from the University of Massachusetts at Amherst, women are just better at it—more accurate at hammering—than are men. And this was not just an assessment of who reported more injuries, either—this was the result of a true battle of the sexes in the lab. "We filmed how subjects hammered, and how close the subject hammered to the target was an index of accuracy," said the study's leader, Duncan Irschick (as reported by the online magazine *LiveScience*). The researchers gathered a group of male and female subjects, gave them hammers, and told them to pound on a mechanical plate that measured force and accuracy. It had different-size targets on it, some big, others smaller, to represent large and small nail heads. On average women were 10 percent more accurate than men . . . in the light.

That's right, in the light. Apparently the men were more accurate hammerers in the all-important hammering in the pitch-black competition (maybe the Handyman Olympics equivalent of curling?). Irschick said that the difference could be based on men and women having different hammering strategies: perhaps men favor force over accuracy and women the opposite? But then he admitted that "If this were true, men should always be less accurate than women, which is not what occurs." Irschick's theory? "Men and women differ in their ability to perceive objects in light versus dark environments, and this has a subsequent effect on motor control."

Maybe. But since when is hammering in the dark a relevant skill in everyday life? Maybe when you lose power in the house? But while women may be better with a hammer (in the light), that is not to say that they will want to take the lead when it comes to the duties where a hammer is required. I am sure that this study would not have shown that women get anywhere near the adrenaline rush that men do with that box of nails (though pain *does* fuel adrenaline, so maybe that rush is just from all those sore thumbs).

CHAPTER 7

Women Are Better Video Gamers

Video games are a waste of time for men with nothing else to do.

—RAY BRADBURY, SALON.COM

Video games and gamers have always been hounded by stereotypes. Back in the era of Atari, Nintendo and, at its storied zenith, Super Nintendo, the typical gamer was unkempt and unlicensed to drive. His forehead was an asteroid shower of acne, and he was completely terrified of girls. He was, of course, also a boy. As far as the stereotype is concerned, gamers are still, stereotypically, carbuncular nerds. But the stereotype has also widened as the technology has gotten slicker to accommodate pro athletes, amateur athletes, and rock star wannabes. This is the *Halo* generation of gamers.

These stereotypes—the dude at leisure, gunning down Martians; the nerd in puberty, frolicking on toadstools—have two things in common. They both imply gaming is a masculine kick, and this may be inaccurate.

In late 2009, a University of Southern California study into the different gaming patterns of the genders revealed that female gamers played, on average, three more hours weekly than their male counterparts, twenty-nine hours to twenty-six. The test case was of a game called *EverQuest II.* Not only were women playing this game with comparable intensity; they were, presumably, outlasting, out-undersleeping, and out-failing-to-shower even the nerdy boys. *They had become the nerds.*

This astonishing news has since been supplemented and confirmed by still more intergalactic revelations. Social online gaming, in which users intimately inhabit an avatar in online communities, is the latest paradigm to transfix the gaming world. It also seems to be primarily a ladies' affair. According to a study run by PopCap Games, a Seattle-based gaming development company, 55 percent of US social gamers are women. In the UK, that number rises to 60 percent. In addition to owning the majority of the gaming demographic, women are also more likely to be hardcore about it. Thirty-eight percent of female social gamers have an "avid" gaming habit (they play multiple times daily, for significant periods of time), whereas only 29 percent of men do the same. The crowning detail? The typical gamer, statistically, in the US and UK alike, is a *forty-three-year-old woman.*

And unlike men, women who decide to dedicate so much of their time to gaming see no adverse effects on their temperament. In fact, the USC study also found that women displayed greater sociability and general well-being during their gaming binges, despite being able to extend those binges for longer. Why? One reason may be that women are biologically wired to have a greater tolerance for the addictive effects of gaming. According to a study by Stanford School of Medicine conducted in 2008, video games activate the part of the brain that makes these games satisfying at a much more intense rate in men than in women. In other words, the mental payoff is larger for guys, making it more difficult to put the controller down. Women are actually, according to a 2007 Harris Interactive survey, two to three times less likely to develop video game addiction. The fact that their brains simply take video games less seriously could have much to do with it.

So not only have women conquered the world of social online gaming, taken the lead in the more classic (and hardcore) types of games, and shown a video game stamina male nerds could only dream of, but they have a neurological advantage that helps keep them, well, more normal. Does all of this make them better than men? Or just better geeks? I'm not sure. But it sure does dispel another myth/stereotype.

CHAPTER 8

Women Appreciate a Good Joke Better

*Nothing spoils a romance so much as
a sense of humor in the woman and the
want of one in a man.*

—OSCAR WILDE

Most guys seem to believe that many of the hilarious moments in life are exclusively reserved for them and their male friends: think *Animal House, The Hangover, Superbad* ... the list goes on and on. *Vanity Fair* even published an article by Christopher Hitchens entitled "Why Women Aren't Funny"—and no, it's not from the 1920s or even 1950s, but from 2007.

Maybe men are funnier, so I figured there might be some empirical evidence to prove it. I came across a 2007 *Daily Telegraph* article that blared "Scientist Claims Men Are Funnier Than Women." It seemed I had found the holy grail: a scientifically sound study that definitively proved that men are the bigger and better jokers. The evidence? Research Professor Sam Shuster of Norwalk and Norwich University Hospital rode around on a unicycle to see who would make fun of him most. Yes, really.

The first line of the piece reads, "Men are more naturally funny than women, according to a male scientist who says men make more jokes and the gags tend to be more aggressive." Huh? One of the side-splitting comments made by those Chris Rock wannabes: "Lost your wheel?" Ha! I know; I was in tears after that one too.

I am not surprised that more men were obnoxious to the guy on the weird-looking bike, but how does that make men funnier? Then came the truly hilarious moment from the article, which explained the phenomenon:

> Dr Nick Neave, a psychologist at the University of Northumbria who has studied the physical, behavioural and psychological effects of testosterone, said men might respond aggressively because they see the other unicycling man as a threat, attracting female attention away from themselves. "This would be particularly challenging for young males entering the breeding market. It does not surprise me that their responses were the more threatening," he said.

Right. There's nothing that gets childbearing women hotter than a dorky researcher, probably clad in short shorts, crouched on a one-wheeler cruising the town.

Meanwhile, there is real evidence—a Stanford University study—showing that women appreciate a good joke more than men. In 2005, a group of women and men were shown a series of cartoons.

They rated them for funniness while an MRI identified the active areas of their brains. Bottom line: the women got more of a buzz out of the cartoons; their brains were literally more rewarded by a funny joke than were men's.

Why? Apparently the women came in with lower expectations. When a woman's brain encountered the punch line, her reward center lit up more than a man's, according to Dr. Allan Reiss, one of the authors of the study: "Women appeared to have less expectation of a reward, which in this case was the punch line of the cartoon. So when they got to the joke's punch line, they were more pleased about it."

Rather than hearing about this and simply accepting that maybe women appreciate a laugh better than men do, Hitchens in that *Vanity Fair* piece wrote: "Slower to get it, more pleased when they do . . . and remember, this is women when confronted with humor. Is it any wonder that they are backward in generating it?"

Maybe he was one of the guys cracking some doozies when Professor Shuster hilariously cruised by on that single-wheel bike.

CHAPTER 9

Women Are Better Gamblers

Someone once asked me why women don't gamble as much as men do, and I gave the common-sensical reply that we don't have as much money. That was a true but incomplete answer. In fact, women's total instinct for gambling is satisfied by marriage.

—GLORIA STEINEM

"In the poker game of life, women are the rake." We owe this fetching analogy to Worm (a.k.a. Edward Norton), No Limit Hold 'Em expert of the 1998 film *Rounders*. (Scuzzy and scheming, Worm is also its premier sleazebag.) Intended to console and inspire his friend, who, having just been dumped, is feeling defeated (which men do more than women after a breakup—see Chapter 1). Worm's words of wisdom, of course, suggest that women don't gamble and don't risk their money. They wait on the sidelines while men, dauntless and debonair, dare the odds in quest of a fortune. When that fortune gets doled out and the losers are sifted from the winners—*that's* when women make their grasping, predictable play.

Alas, in the poker game of life, Worm, it would seem, is the guy who bets his roll on a bad hunch—then gets tossed for bad behavior. (He's also the guy, needless to say, without a girlfriend.) In a comprehensive 2007 study of 40,499 online gamblers conducted by the Cambridge Health Alliance, an organization affiliated with Harvard Medical School, women exhibited "more effective sports gambling behavior than men," according to Richard LaBrie, the study's author.

The study, which culled its results from giant databases, shows that women are more aggressive in their bets, more rapid-fire in placing them, and more likely to turn a profit at the tables. While men wagered an average of eleven euros per bet, women wagered an average of fifteen. Women also placed wagers over 15 percent more frequently than men—earning them nicely proportional 15 percent greater winnings.

Women were therefore both the exemplars and the beneficiaries of a broader truth brought home by the study: that the bigger, bolder bettors are 50 percent less prone to lose money than the smaller, more tentative bettors. So not only do women gamble. Not only do women do well gambling at tables, rather than, as in the stereotype, staying primly to the side at the slots. They are *braver* gamblers—and they profit by it.

That does not mean that you will see *more* women at the tables, but it does mean that the house may want to train the internal cameras on them. The old truth survives that you have to have guts to gamble, but maybe the shorthand for that should refer to having ovarios rather than cojones.

CHAPTER 10

Women Get Ready
Faster Than Men

*If a girl looks swell when she meets
you, who gives a damn if she's late?
Nobody.*

—HOLDEN CAULFIELD, *THE CATCHER IN THE RYE*

I am a lawyer, and so this book is filled with evidence—comprehensive studies, facts, and statistics—that shows that women are better (sometimes far better) than men in so many ways. In some cases, the findings may seem surprising, but the evidence and science behind them are clear. Well, this one may not be quite as definitive. I am not going to challenge the findings, and other more comprehensive studies in this book have shown that women tend to be more efficient and goal-oriented, but I'll admit that I wonder whether maybe, just maybe, this could be a rogue survey.

A company called Superdrug, the second-largest purveyor of health and beauty products in Great Britain, surveyed three thousand Brits in 2010 and found that, contrary to expectations, men spend more time getting ready to go out than women. The guys said they took an average of eighty-three minutes per day to clean, shave, style their hair, moisturize, choose clothes, etc. (Are that many guys moisturizing? I thought I was one of the few?)

Women, on the other hand, did their presumably more exhaustive hair, clothes, and makeup routine four minutes faster, in just seventy-nine minutes. There is always a possibility that the time estimates could be skewed based on the difference between time spent on one's image versus time spent getting ready to leave the house— maybe women do their moisturizing at night, for example—but that still doesn't account for another interesting finding in the study: the girls spent only pennies more per month on grooming products, no matter what time of day they intended to use them. Could it be that British dudes just preen more than us Yankees?

The not-that-surprising part of the survey: men spent an average of twenty-three minutes in the shower—a minute longer than women. OK, but that leaves about sixty minutes out of the eighty-three unaccounted for in the morning routine. Question: what exactly are guys doing for that entire hour after the leisurely shower?

A spokesperson for Superdrug provided a social explanation for the time difference: "Once upon a time, it was cool for men to appear rough and ready, looking like they hadn't spent more than a couple of minutes getting ready in a morning. But these days, everyone appreciates a man who takes care of his appearance, smells nice and looks like he has made an effort."

Made an effort? Yes. Looks like he made an effort? I'm not so sure.

PART II

WOMEN
ARE
SMARTER

CHAPTER 11

Women Have Better Memories

*Women always worry about the things
that men forget; men always worry
about the things women remember.*

—AUTHOR UNKNOWN

"Honey, where did I leave my wallet?"

It's a common refrain in households around America—men pleading with women to help them recall faces, names, dates: you name it. But it's not just poor dad getting scolded for forgetting to take out the trash or call his mother (or, umm, mother-in-law). It turns out there's a reason why "men forget everything; women remember everything" is a classic entry in any anthology of grandma's wisdom: women are better equipped to retain information, and there's an evolutionary explanation for that.

But first, the facts: Several studies now prove that women have a more developed ability to recall information. The most recent comes from the University of London, where a series of memory tests were performed in March 2010. The study, conducted on middle-aged men and women, involved verbal memory. Subjects listened to ten words at a time. In the first round of testing, they were given two minutes to remember as many as possible. In the second, they were asked to recall the words five minutes later without hearing them a second time. The women beat out their male counterparts by 5 percent in the first test and 8 percent in the second.

OK, so they can remember more words. It's great to know that girls might better recite poems in high school, but that skill just seems so . . . wordy. How relevant could that be to the real world after they take their SATs? How about this: girls aren't just better with words; they are also better at recognizing faces.

A study released in June 2010 by Toronto's York University concluded that women are better able to recall faces after seeing them for the first time. Male and female subjects were given twenty seconds to memorize a series of faces, which were later shuffled in with faces not previously shown to them. The women scored 5 percent higher than men. That means 5 percent fewer women have to fake it at a meeting with someone they should remember.

Given that they're better at remembering both words and faces, it should be no surprise that women are also the more advanced gender at what scientists call "episodic memory." A 2008 study conducted in Sweden and cited by ScienceDaily.com found that women trounced men in their ability to remember the totality of everyday events, including words, objects, and pictures.

So why are women so much better at retaining information in both the short and long terms? According to psychologist David

Geary from the University of Missouri in Columbia, it's all about evolutionary head-to-head competition among females. A better memory not only makes it easier to keep track of suitable mates, but it helps with keeping track of potential rivals, Geary told *Scientific American*. "Women certainly fought and continue to fight over the best guys . . . those with good genes and resources to invest in kids. Remembering details of personal experiences is important for monitoring and maneuvering relationships, including disrupting the social and romantic ties of other women who are competitors."

Whatever the reason, you women might want to show some pity and take it easy on the menfolk when they forget an anniversary, the name of your sister, or where they left the keys. Maybe it's not that they don't care as much; it may just be that biology dictates they simply can't do it as well as you.

CHAPTER 12

Women Are Better Investors

October. This is one of the peculiarly dangerous months to speculate in stocks. The others are July, January, September, April, November, May, March, June, December, August and February.

—MARK TWAIN,
PUDD'NHEAD WILSON'S CALENDAR FOR 1894

A 2010 *New York* magazine feature on women in the stock market described a "spontaneous and slightly goofy" conversation among seasoned stock analysts over the fall of Lehman Brothers, the largest bankruptcy in American history. Looking back on the times before the stock market crash, the group figured that the bank should have hired more women. In fact, they concluded that if the firm had been "Lehman Sisters," it would probably still be in business. They may not have even realized how true that was.

Wall Street as we know it is a sort of Darwinian experiment where greed is good, audacity is better, and the stock market is just an inevitable conclusion to a *Lord of the Flies*–esque experiment that gives a cabal of young, adventurous boys the reins. A 2010 report from the *Hedge Fund Journal* revealed that out of the $1.5 trillion invested in hedge funds around the world, only 3 percent was being managed by women. It's a shame, because the average levelheaded woman may be able to blow away the profits of most of those boys.

The fact that women tend to be better investors would hardly be a surprise to biologists. There's an entire academic body of literature dedicated to the many ways in which women, who are more risk averse, are better able to maintain a successful portfolio and/or get the most out of their stocks. A 2009 *Wall Street Journal* piece entitled "For Mother's Day, Give Her the Reins to the Portfolio" lists the results several researchers found in observing women in the market. For example, they cited a 2001 survey of investors in New York which found that 92 percent of women said that incomplete or vague information made them wary of risk, while just 69 percent of men said the same, and men traded their stocks 50 percent more often than women. In fact, it translated into women's returns beating men's by one full percentage point a year—and that was years before the recession really hit Wall Street.

In March 2010, the *New York Times* reported that women were making and keeping more money in the stock market than men. Not only did the article show men more willing to take incomplete information into consideration when trading, but in an effort to avoid losing money, men were buying and selling like crazy, making their portfolios that much more volatile. And if that is not bad enough, according to a 2009 study by the mutual fund company Vanguard, men were also much more likely to sell their shares at the wrong time, upping their losses. The *Times* explained, "Those sales presumably meant big losses—and missing the start of the market rally that began a year ago." The head of Vanguard elaborated: "Male investors, as a group, appear to be overconfident," leading them to buy or sell without all of the necessary information, while women are more likely to wait until they know more.

It's not just American women either. A study published by the BBC and conducted by a group called Digital Look examined male and female portfolios between 2003 and 2004. The average woman's portfolio rose 10 percent—three points higher than the rise of the entire market, and four higher than the average man's. Again, the study attributed the success of female investors to avoiding risky bets as well as to their tendency to keep their portfolios more balanced with a stronger emphasis on a company's reputation rather than recent statistics, which guys seem to love.

The results are so pronounced that apparently there is a new trend to bring out the girly side of the men working on Wall Street. The *New York* magazine feature details how investment coaches are trying to get stockbrokers in touch with their "feminine side" before heading to the trading floor—things like writing their feelings in diaries and, in one case, a boss allegedly forcing a trader to take female hormones. Shockingly, none of these seem to work as well as just, well, getting a woman to do this typically masculine job. We'll probably have to wait for an entirely new body of research and studies to show that shooting a guy up with estrogen is less effective (and, more important, less cost effective!) than just sending a girl to the trading room floor.

CHAPTER 13

Women Are Better at Faking Attraction

*You will be amused when you see that I
have more than once deceived without
the slightest qualm of conscience,
both knaves and fools.*

—GIACOMO CASANOVA

How many times have you seen or heard about an overconfident
(and often, umm, cheesy) young man talking about how "into me"
a woman is? Think guys like Mike "The Situation" Sorrentino of
Jersey Shore infamy. It could be the result of a cursory glance across
a room or a polite smile at a bar as she attempts to get him out of
the way while beelining to the nearest ladies' room. Even an "xoxo"
signature at the bottom of an e-mail is sufficient for some guys to
become convinced "I am in." One thing is for sure: time and again,
guys walk away with the often mistaken impression that she is totally enamored. This as many women pore over books and advice

columns purporting to serve as wake-up calls of just the opposite: that for whatever reason "He is just *not* that into you."

Well, it's time for men to realize that the key difference may be that women are just more convincing in their efforts to be polite, meaning they pretend more—and better—than do guys. And we're not just talking about Meg Ryan enthusiastically faking an orgasm in a Jewish deli in *When Harry Met Sally* . . . Remember that even the most adept of men at the mating game, like "The Situation," get blindsided as he did by Sammi "Sweetheart" when she went for Ronnie instead (OK, no more *Jersey Shore* references).

In 2009, Indiana University conducted a study where college-aged men and women were asked to watch video clips of couples interacting on "speed dates"—singles meeting a large number of prospective dates in successive and quick one-on-one conversations. Each observer watched twenty-four videos of different men and women interacting, then rated whether he or she thought the man seemed interested in the woman and vice versa. The male and female participants' assessments were pretty even, with both accurately guessing the interest level of the men, while both the men and women in the study consistently overstated the interest level of the women. Bottom line: for whatever reason, the women fooled everyone.

"The hardest-to-read women were being misperceived at a much higher rate than the hardest-to-read men. Those women were being flirtatious, but it turned out they weren't interested at all," said lead author Skyler Place, a doctoral student at Indiana University in Bloomington. "Nobody could really read what these deceptive females were doing, including other women."

In five of the twenty-four videos, 80 percent of the participants got it wrong, mistakenly thinking those "deceptive females" were interested in guys with whom they were chatting. Those women, it turns out, were just being friendly and had no romantic interest.

As relationships develop, it seems either women remain tougher to read or, more likely, men just don't pay as close attention to their partners (the above study might indicate that they figure she is just so "into me" that it doesn't really matter). A study from The Hebrew University of Jerusalem showed that women actually know and understand their partners far better than do men.

In that study, ninety-seven couples in the US, married and unmarried, aged eighteen to forty-six, answered a series of questions about their relationships—and the women were consistently and significantly more accurate when describing the perceptions and desires of their partners. Maybe that's why the women always seemed to be so much better than their partners on that old TV show *The Newlywed Game*, where Bob Eubanks made them answer random personal questions about leaving the toilet seat up or "making whoopee" (though, as far as I know, there have been no scientific studies on *Newlywed Game* accuracy rates).

So it seems the guys are proving to be a bit more clueless both before and during a relationship. They more often mistakenly believe women are interested in them romantically, and when women are, men don't seem to really know why. Maybe Snooki was right when she said it'd be easier to just date other women, after all (OK, I'll *really* stop now).

CHAPTER 14

Women Are Better at Avoiding Internet Fraud

On behalf of the Trustees and Executor of the Estate of Late Luciano Pavarotti, I hereby attempt to reach you again. I wish to notify you that Late Luciano Pavarotti made you a beneficiary to his will. He left the sum of ten Million five Hundred Thousand Dollars… Please you should fill the information below for more clearities and identification of your information we have here.

—SPAM E-MAIL

Do you ever peek into your e-mail account's spam folder and wonder who still falls for this stuff? The highly resistible wiles of various Nigerian princes; dizzyingly cheap Canadian pharmacy prices for male enhancement; subject lines like "Your debts could make you rich!," "Sapphire Russian Marriage," and "!!!!!!!" The truth is plenty of people still fall for these scams. Well, actually, plenty of men do.

According to the FBI's Internet Crime Complaint Center (ICCC), a much larger number of men fall for online cons than women. Every year the ICCC releases crime reports with demographic analysis, and year after year men top the list in both perpetrating and falling victim to internet crimes. In 2009, 54 percent of all victims were male, and among all victims men also lost more money (about fifty-one cents more per man than woman scammed).

The report also describes the most common scams, and, predictably, they are targeted at men (with the exception of, maybe, "free astrological readings"). Typical scams range from organizations like "Ishmael Ghost Islamic Group" threatening a family member and requesting money in exchange for safety to "free" trials of computer virus protection software aimed at businesspeople. But by far the most common scams use the effect of the economic recession to target people who have recently been laid off (which is happening more to men—see Chapter 35).

One scam even used the voice of President Barack Obama to direct recently laid-off workers to a website that guaranteed no-strings-attached stimulus money. Others promise stay-at-home jobs that require social security info in exchange for nonexistent wages. And yes, those wealthy foreign royalty e-mails do convince some people to share their banking information—though they've become less effective since their peak in 2006 when "the Nigerian letter scam ... on average bilked each complainant of $5,100. Check fraud came in second, pulling in an average of $3,744 per victim," according to *Network Computing*.

That's not to say that women don't fall for scams too—they are still about 26 percent more likely to be the victims of traditional, as opposed to online, identity theft. So why the divergent results online? ICCC researcher John Kane (quoted in *CSO* magazine) argued that "Historically, men were more apt to purchase large ticket items like electronics . . . that could explain a lot of it . . . Men tend to fall victim . . . to business investment schemes and some other schemes that have a higher dollar loss." Online, women are apparently more cautious and less tempted by certain frauds.

There is also the fact that a higher number of online criminals are men, so they might understand the male psyche better. The variance could also be a direct result of still unexplained differences in male and female online behaviors, rather than the behavior of the criminals. Either way, it's a sad reality that the cliché of grandma getting conned by an unscrupulous online scam is probably less likely than it happening to gramps.

CHAPTER 15

Women Are Better Students

The people I'm getting furious with are the women's liberationists. They keep getting on their soapboxes proclaiming that women are brighter than men. That's true, but it should be kept quiet or it ruins the whole racket.

—ANITA LOOS

When you picture the student whose notes everyone wants to borrow, what does she look like? She. From movies to real life it seems that it's often the girl with the excellent handwriting and attendance record who serves as the "teacher's pet." Well now, it's increasingly becoming clear that there is good reason for that.

At our colleges and universities, men are increasingly coming to embody a slacker underclass. According to the Bureau of Labor

Statistics, colleges graduate 185 women for every 100 men. That means men are graduating college at a trifling 54 percent of the rate that women are. In a recent projection, the Department of Education anticipated that by 2016, 61 percent of bachelor's degrees, 63 percent of master's degrees, and 58 percent of doctoral degrees will go to women as well.

In a *New York Times* piece called, tellingly, "At Colleges, Women Are Leaving Men in the Dust," Department of Education statistics cited show that men, whatever their race or socioeconomic group, are less likely than women to get bachelor's degrees—and among those who do, fewer complete their degrees in four or five years.

And it's not just that there are more women; they're doing better as well. How much better? Well, let's start by comparing the smartest of the smarty-pants. At Harvard University in 2006, more than 55 percent of women graduated with honors compared with only 50 percent of men. Throw in the fact that there are significantly more women at Harvard (and at universities across the country), and you have a whole lot more women graduating with honors than men.

Are women just smarter? More committed students? According to the 2005 National Survey of Student Engagement, which reported results from 90,000 students at 530 postsecondary institutions, male university students are significantly more inclined to relax or socialize (eleven hours weekly, to be precise). Linda Sax, in her book *The Gender Gap in College*, similarly found that collegiate men are more likely to skip class, turn assignments in late, or just drop out than collegiate women. Some sociologists attribute this to an old-fashioned idea of masculinity that still wields a lot of cultural clout: the man as brash, irreverent, and above doing his homework.

Others have speculated that the difference could be connected to the fact that women are better multitaskers. In July 2010, the *Telegraph* reported on a study from the University of Hertfordshire in England in which fifty men and fifty women were challenged to complete three tasks (solving math problems, locating restaurants on a map, and finding a lost key) simultaneously. They also got a trivia question phone call while they balanced the three tasks. The women beat the men in a landslide—70 percent of women outperformed their male counterparts (maybe because men had no idea where to begin finding the key).

The gender imbalance at universities has become so pronounced that in 2010 the *New York Times* reported that some Ivy League schools have been accused of stacking the deck in favor of the boys in an effort to level the playing field:

[A]t some schools, efforts to balance the numbers have been met with complaints that less-qualified men are being admitted over more-qualified women. In December, the United States Commission on Civil Rights moved to subpoena admissions data from 19 public and private colleges to look at whether they were discriminating against qualified female applicants.

Wow. Accusations of affirmative action policies—*for men.* That kind of says it all.

CHAPTER 16

Women Are Better at Social Media

I'm a '70s mom, and my daughter is a '90s mom. I know a lot of women my age who are real computer freaks.

—FLORENCE HENDERSON,
A.K.A. *THE BRADY BUNCH*'S CAROL BRADY

Imagine calling the Geek Squad or some other "please fix my computer" service and seeing two women emerge from the run-down van. You might be a bit surprised—maybe pleasantly so. After all, the greater computer geek world is not universally recognized as a particularly attractive place for women. Take a quick look around the world of online social networking and you'll only find a handful of girls among the "titans" of the industry, who tend to be mostly young cyber-entrepreneur guys in hoodies: Facebook's Mark Zuckerberg, Twitter's Evan Williams, or Foursquare's Dennis Crowley. Read some quick statistics on any social network and you'll find that men tend to be more popular on them as well. According to research by the *Harvard Business Review* in June 2009, men have an average of 15 percent more followers than women on Twitter. But the Twitter numbers only tell us at face value that men tend to link with other men, and women tend to link with ... men.

As with so many other categories where women excel despite lower expectations, female users of social networks both outnumber and outperform their male counterparts. In terms of absolute use and proficiency, there's little doubt women rule social media.

It starts when girls are young, and not necessarily on the internet. A UK group called Tesco Computers for Schools conducted a study on computer proficiency and gender at a very early age and, according to the BBC, the results showed an abundantly clear gap between the abilities of girls and boys to perform basic tasks on a computer. Conducted in February 2008, the study looked at skills such as creating documents, using search engines, and, with older subjects, creating social networking profiles. Among seven-year-olds, 73 percent of girls could use search engines and 62 percent could edit documents, significantly higher numbers than for the boys. (I am sure those seven-year-old girls could, in this regard, shame many titans of industry as well.) And while one in ten boys felt a lack of confidence around computers, only 6 percent of girls expressed the same insecurity.

Beyond basic computer skills, women also excel at using the internet to connect and communicate with others. Another, newer study conducted by the research network comScore, Inc., in May 2010 examined the social networking habits of adult men and women and found a six percentage point difference between social networking use among the sexes. Reported in the *Silicon Valley/*

San Jose Business Journal, the study found that 76 percent of women with internet access across the globe said they had visited a social networking site, compared with 70 percent of men. Women are also better acquainted with them, accounting for 57 percent of the total time spent by people on these sites—meaning they spend significantly more time browsing and using the sites. On average, the study found that women spend about an hour and a half more per month on social networking sites than men.

So what are they doing on these sites for so much longer? Surely it can't take women any longer than men to understand Facebook's new privacy settings (maybe they have more to hide?). The UK *Times* tried to answer this question, but not before adding even more evidence to the overwhelming pile: They reported on a Pew Research Center study that found that 70 percent of teenage girls have social networking profiles, compared to 57 percent of teenage boys. Girls are also 5 percent more likely to have a blog, and 10 percent more likely to have a personal website. The *Times*'s explanation: "There is widespread agreement that the prime driver behind the enthusiastic uptake of the internet by young girls is their desire to gossip." Which may just go to show women can't even catch a break when there is overwhelming evidence for them simply being more engaged or better at something than men.

John Horrigan, a representative of the Pew Research Center, declined to echo the sentiments in the *Times*'s report, though he may have been making the same point: "The internet is a very expressive medium and you're looking at times in a girl's life when they are very socially expressive." At least part of that is true: one can express oneself on the internet, and women do tend to have more proficient communications skills, which make them, among other things, better students (see the previous chapter)—this despite the fact that they may also be procrastinating more online.

But there's another theory, which both Horrigan and the *Times* seem to be resisting: maybe, just maybe, women are better with technology, or have found a more significant use for it than men. Perhaps there still isn't a female majority in the more purely technical computer science fields, but in the much more accessible social technologies that are beginning to define a generation and will be a necessary skill for so many jobs in this decade, women have shown that their prowess is more than just idle gossip.

PART III

WOMEN ARE BETTER CITIZENS

CHAPTER 17

Women Are Better Drivers

*I like to drive with my knees.
Otherwise, how can I put on my lipstick
and talk on the phone?*

—SHARON STONE

"Women drivers." There may be no more pervasive sexist cliché than the one that suggests a woman behind the wheel is an inherent danger. Maybe apart from "Sunday drivers," the ladies have long been the prime target for reckless cabbies, angry truck drivers, and chauvinists nationwide. Delays, accidents, and traffic jams simply must be the result of some oblivious woman applying lipstick at the wheel.

Bam!—another myth shattered. And I'm not just talking about NASCAR sensation Danica Patrick (although she is pretty cool). A 2007 Carnegie Mellon University study showed that, based on the number of miles driven, male drivers have a 77 percent higher risk of dying in a car accident than women. In fact, the male author of the study was quoted as saying that when his wife takes the wheel: "I put a mitt in my mouth and ride shotgun."

Per 100 million trips, estimated fatalities were 14.61 for men to just 6.53 for women. And according to the Insurance Institute for Highway Safety, 14,512 male drivers died in 2007 as compared to 5,865 females.

In New York City—one of the most difficult places to drive in America—a 2010 city traffic study found that over the previous five years, 80 percent of all crashes where pedestrians were seriously injured or killed involved men behind the wheel—and no, 80 percent of all drivers are not male. Seth Solomonow, a spokesman for the city's transportation department, told the *New York Times* that the imbalance "is far too great to be explained away by the predominance of men among bus, livery, taxi and delivery drivers."

The superiority of women behind the wheel is not limited to taking the kids to Little League either. Some mass transit companies, recognizing that women tend to be safer and take better care of their vehicles, are actually taking the initiative to hire more women drivers. In fact, one of the largest bus operators in Sydney, Australia, successfully petitioned the government for an exception to their antidiscrimination laws, which prohibit companies from hiring employees based on gender. According to Sydney's *Daily Telegraph*, the company, Veolia Transport, made the case that its employees were disproportionately male but, more important, it felt more comfortable leaving its fleets in the hands of women because they believed they simply made better bus drivers. According to the company's managing director, "We find women are gentler on the buses, on the machinery, than men, and they relate to passengers better." The government of Australia agreed to allow them to discriminate against men.

So what makes women drivers safer? Well, maybe it's because men get more tickets, have more accidents, and drive drunk far more often. Translation: women are far more careful drivers. It's a difference so stark that it now translates into lower insurance rates for the entire gender. An assessment of 300,000 quotes by Insurance .com showed women being quoted lower premiums than men by an average of 7.3 percent: $1,710 per year for females versus $1,824 for males.

Sure, there are other relevant factors such as age, time of day, and the type of ride you choose. But hey, generalities and stereotypes have defined female drivers for years, so now that the numbers are in, it's at least fair to speculate that a traffic mishap is likely the result of those damn "men drivers."

CHAPTER 18

Women in Politics Are Less Corrupt

The reason there are so few female politicians is that it is too much trouble to put makeup on two faces.

—MAUREEN MURPHY,
CHAIRWOMAN OF THE COOK COUNTY REPUBLICAN PARTY

American cartoonist Kin Hubbard once said, "We'd all like to vote for the best man, but he's never a candidate." So we vote for the candidate we get—most often a man in a suit promising never to cheat the people he represents.

But from Boss Tweed to Spiro Agnew to Jack Abramoff, almost all of America's great political crooks have been masculine figures. And no, it's not just that women have only recently been allowed to participate in our national sport, nor is it that our most fascinating and prominent political villains are guys. Several studies on corruption in governments across the planet have shown that the more female legislators, the more honest the *legislature.*

In 1999, researchers at the World Bank Development Research Group analyzed data from dozens of countries' parliaments looking for a connection between gender and corruption. They started with previous research that showed women tend to score higher on "integrity tests" and are more passionate about "defending ethical behavior," which is all a fancy way of saying that women are more likely to say they are honest than men. I can just hear it now from John, Steve, and Bill: "Well at least the guys fessed up about lying!"

Yeah, yeah—but women's actions speak louder than their words. The World Bank team took account of the corruption level within the individual countries and even the social and economic development of each and found "a strong, negative, and statistically significant relationship between the proportion of women in a country's legislature and the level of corruption." Fewer women meant more corruption.

So what exactly did "corruption" mean? Selling a Senate seat, trading a vote for fund-raising, having an Imelda Marcos–style shoe closet? The study kept it simple: ". . . the likelihood that government officials will demand special payments and the extent to which illegal payments are expected throughout low levels of government."

A year later, another team from the Williams College Center for Development Economics conducted a ninety-three-country survey to answer the same question. In this one, they went even further to level the playing field between poor and more developed countries by making sure they accounted for things such as culture, religion, and education levels. Again, they came to the same conclusion: "Countries which have greater representation of women in government or in market work have lower levels of corruption" and "There is indeed a gender differential in tolerance for corruption." The countries in which women had the most profound effect on keeping down corruption were Sweden, the Netherlands, and Estonia.

But maybe when more of them get that taste of the political power nectar they too will become more corrupt? Not so, according to the Williams study. In the United States, there has not been a significant increase in corruption among female politicians in the past few decades despite a clear increase in the number of women in politics, and more generally, they found "large differentials have persisted despite the increase in women's participation in the labor force."

So next time a sourpuss bemoans the fact that "all politicians are crooks," it might be worth lifting his or her spirits by pointing out that it's really only men behaving badly and that, despite the advances women have made in the workforce and the political world, their reputation is still as clean (at least by political standards) as it was when Americans elected the first female governor in 1925 (Wyoming's Nellie Tayloe Ross).

The campaign ad of the future: Vote for me because I'm ... well, because I'm not a guy.

CHAPTER 19

Women Have Better Bathroom Manners

*Men who consistently leave
the toilet seat up secretly want
women to get up to go to the
bathroom in the middle of the
night and fall in.*

—RITA RUDNER

There's an old joke that has been told by (male) Yale alums for years. It's about how a Harvard man and a Yale man spot one another at a urinal, then finish and zip up. The Harvard man proceeds to the sink to wash his hands, while the Yale man immediately makes for the exit. The Harvard man says, "At Harvard they teach us to wash our hands after we urinate." The Yale man replies, "At Yale they teach us not to piss on our hands." Yuk yuk yuk. Yeah, it's not exactly a knee-slapper, but it's the sort of defense/excuse that I'm guessing many men would use when confronted with the evidence showing how much more sanitary women are than men in bathrooms.

The most recent study comes from the London School of Hygiene & Tropical Medicine (I know, I know—there's a school of hygiene?). They used sensors to assess how much soap was being used and the numbers are staggering. Out of 250,000 people, 32 percent of men used soap compared with 64 percent of women. Eww. So do guys need to be reminded that washing with soap helps prevent disease? Well, apparently even that doesn't really work so well. The study also found that while women responded to reminders like "Water doesn't kill germs, soap does," men needed to be totally disgusted to change behavior with signs such as "Soap it off or eat it later." Yum.

Believe it or not, more than one study has been conducted on gender-related bathroom etiquette with consistent results. Penn State "researchers" found that public bathroom signs that say "Please wash hands" led many women to use soap and water, but did not change men's hand-washing (or lack thereof) behavior.

Yet another study, from the Soap and Detergent Association, which spied on six thousand people in four big American cities in 2007, found that a third of guys didn't wash after using the bathroom, compared with 12 percent of women. I'm sure all those guys would suddenly become "Yalies" if confronted, claiming that they are not spraying their hands. Well, I wonder how all the guys whose hands they're shaking would feel about the matter? Finally, on a gender-neutral and somewhat nauseating note, a 2010 Harris Interactive poll found 82 percent of people say they "always" wash their hands after changing a diaper.

Please. If you are one of the 18 percent who do not, a heads-up would be nice.

CHAPTER 20

Women Are Better at Giving and Following Directions

Men read maps better than women because only men can understand the concept of an inch equaling a hundred miles.

—ROSEANNE BARR

How many times have you seen, or heard about, or been in a car with, men refusing to ask for directions? It's about as old a cliché as a bunch of pals sitting around watching a game, eating nachos, and drinking "brewskis." When lost, a woman will supposedly want to stop at a gas station or ask a local for some amount of guidance, while the man would prefer to drive in circles for long periods of time rather than admit that he needs assistance. To make matters worse for everyone in the car, research now shows that the boys might actually need more help in getting places than the girls do, since women are better at giving, taking, and remembering directions, including on highways.

A May 2010 study conducted by St. Joseph's University in Philadelphia placed two groups of thirty men and women at various gas stations and watched them give passersby directions—the goal of the study being to figure out which gender was better at giving directions to strangers, not just which is better at getting from one place to another. The passersby asking for directions were actually undercover researchers who knew perfectly well how to get to the well-known tourist attractions. The male good Samaritans did not fare well. The researchers noted, "Men included significantly more mileage estimates than females, but their estimates contained more errors."

Not surprisingly, the women were twice as likely as men to "pause significantly" before giving directions and were less likely to guess how long the trip would take. When they did decide to guess, they were much more accurate than men (half of the women were correct, while only a third of the men were). Why the gap? Men were making rash decisions and, well, often just winging it, perhaps to impress the traveler, or perhaps out of simple hubris. Who knows.

When a woman felt she wasn't properly equipped to make distance estimates or indicate the direction of a tourist attraction, she just didn't do it. When a man felt the same, he was far more likely to take a wild guess. Most of those guesses were wrong—or, as the British newspaper the *Telegraph*, which covered the story, put it: "Researchers found that they (women) were more adept than men at telling strangers where to go because they took the time to think the instructions through."

And when it comes to actually following directions, women also have the upper hand. While studies have shown that men and women have different fortes in direction and self-orientation, women appear to be better suited to understand and follow casual directions from a bystander. According to a 2002 study from the University of Saskatchewan, men are better equipped to understand "Euclidean orientation strategies"—cardinal directions, left/right orientation, and exact numerical distances—while women depend more on "environmental information" such as landmarks. This gives women a distinct advantage with the kind of directions you get from a passerby, who is more likely to remember where the local McDonald's is than whether it's 1.3 miles away. Yes, that means that men appear to be better at reading maps, but when it comes to following directions, women come out on top.

So now a woman doesn't only have to worry about getting in a car with a man who will drive less safely than she would (see Chapter 17) and be less likely to admit that he's lost; when asking for directions, she also has to make sure to ask another woman or risk being sent on a wild goose chase by some guy who doesn't really know what he's talking about.

CHAPTER 21

Women Vote More

Sensible and responsible women do not want to vote. The relative positions to be assumed by man and woman in the working out of our civilization were assigned long ago by a higher intelligence than ours.

—GROVER CLEVELAND

Those words from a guy elected president of the United States. Twice. (He was the only one to serve two nonconsecutive terms, the twenty-second and twenty-fourth president). Obviously, these days an attitude like that would have prevented President Cleveland from becoming an assemblyman in Cleveland. And not just because it's overtly sexist; it's also political suicide. Whatever "higher intelligence" handed out the assignments forgot to tell those "sensible and responsible" women that they don't want to vote. In fact, the numbers in America for the past several decades are clear: a higher percentage of women than men vote regularly, making them a more significant political force.

Women have been a bigger presence at election stations—and as such, have had more of a say in dictating who holds public office—for the past four decades and counting. Census data show that since 1964—the first year women voted in higher numbers than men in a national election—they have eclipsed men in sheer numbers at polling stations, averaging several thousands of votes more than their male counterparts. The initial increase is due in part to the fact that women have outnumbered men in general for some time, but in 1980, women also surpassed men in percentage of the population going out to vote, and they have done so in every national election since then.

The numbers in the twenty-first century are more pronounced than ever before, though the statistics show this has had little to do with the candidates, some of whom have been the most prominent American female politicians in history. Apparently women don't just vote because one of their own is on the ballot; women just vote.

In the 2000 presidential election, census data show 61 percent of female registered voters showed up at the polls compared to only 58 percent of guys. The numbers were similar in 2004; 65 percent of women came to the polls, while only 62 percent of men did. This meant that out of all votes in that election, 54 percent came from women. The steady climb continued in 2008, seemingly unaffected by the changing faces of American presidential candidates. Sixty-six percent of women registered to vote showed up, compared to 62 percent of men. That's close to ten thousand more women than men choosing to have a say in the future of the country.

Maybe it's just presidential elections? Or not. The census numbers are similar for midterm elections in this decade as well. In 2002,

47 percent of registered female voters went to the polls, versus 45 percent of men. Sure, the 20 percent drop in voting affects the gap between male and female voting percentages, but not enough to fully diminish the women's lead. In 2006, the same advantage for women: 49 percent of women registered to vote signed in, as opposed to roughly 47 percent of men. And in 2010, according to CNN, 53 percent of those who voted were female, while 47 percent were male.

All of which means it might be time to rethink the focus of political ads. Yes, male names still dominate American election booths (for now), but more women are pulling the levers for them. Actually, it has been that way for the past forty-seven years.

PART IV

WOMEN ARE HEALTH-IER

CHAPTER 22

Women Have Better Muscular Endurance

*Being a woman is of special
interest only to aspiring male
transsexuals. To actual women,
it is simply a good excuse
not to play football.*

—FRAN LEBOWITZ

As I said in my opening statement, I am not going to argue that women are universally faster or stronger than men. They are not. (Although it has been reported that one of the greatest men ever, Abraham Lincoln, at six feet four inches tall, was regularly beaten up by his wife, Mary Todd.) But that doesn't mean that women can't be *better* at certain athletic endeavors—in particular, endurance sports such as long-distance running, where strength is not the primary or determinative factor in success. Sure, the top men run faster than the top women, and that may be the case forever, or for as long as men have longer legs and more forceful muscles. But doesn't it seem like more ordinary women than men run long distances on a regular basis? Maybe they're more committed to losing weight than men—there's a whole division of sociology dedicated to body image that would argue this—but there may be another, less image-conscious explanation: the fact that women are simply better wired for endurance sports.

A University of Colorado study from 2000 showed that, in certain stamina-related exercises, women's endurance was almost twice that of men in the purest terms: exertion over time. Solely in terms of time, the numbers read even more impressively for women: they were able to continue the exercises for about 75 percent longer than men. Were they just trying harder? Nope—that's why the amount of energy exerted is as important in the study as the amount of time spent on the exercise. They weren't performing at a higher percentage of their maximum strength; rather, the variation appears to be a result of fundamental differences between male and female muscles.

This is reflected in the longest and most grueling of competitions, in which women sometimes simply beat the men outright. *Forbes* reported in 2008: "Pamela Reed won the 2002 and 2003 Badwater Ultramarathon, a grueling, 135-mile race through the Mojave Desert. She followed up by becoming the first person—male or female—to run 300 miles straight without sleep. Her male rival Dean Karnazes, who won Badwater in 2004, attempted the 300-mile run twice and failed."

Why would females have an advantage? It may be in their hormones, and even their blood. In 2003 the *Boston Globe* reported:

Estrogen is a disadvantage in muscle development but offers women an edge in endurance. Research suggests estrogen has a protective effect on muscles, making women less prone to soreness. It may also delay fatigue. . . .

A key measure of athletic function relates to how an individual takes oxygen from the air, feeds it into the bloodstream and, in turn, to muscles. . . . Men's larger heart and lungs and higher hemoglobin levels are a boon, but research suggests women have more efficient ways to shunt oxygen-rich blood to help power active muscles.

Specifically with regard to running, the explanation of the differences between the genders may also stem from the same trait that makes women better gamblers (see Chapter 9), investors (see Chapter 12), drivers (see Chapter 17), and even mushroom gatherers (see Chapter 36)— they are just more efficient and think for the long term.

A 2010 article from the *Chicago Tribune* said about long-distance running: "Women are actually better suited for the sport than their male counterparts, Amby Burfoot argues in a revised and updated edition of the *Runner's World Complete Book of Running*. Women tend to pace themselves better at longer distances; studies show men, perhaps fueled by testosterone, go out too hard, too soon and end up bonking more often than women."

There may also be a far simpler explanation and it's the same one that may lead women to run more in the first place: fat. Women tend to have higher percentages of body fat, and layers of fat have been shown to help regulate body temperature in heat and cold. Couple this with the fact that estrogen seems to protect their muscles somewhat from damage, and it's clear how the whole package, while slightly slower, is better equipped for a long trek.

Those advantages may make women more effective cyclers as well. Cycling expert David Balkin reports on the New Hampshire tourism site SeacoastNH.com that women cyclists have the "ideal trifecta: less weight, improved aerodynamics and greater endurance." Women, he argues, do not overpower the bike either: ". . . they sit lighter, pedal more easily and conserve a lot of energy. On a bike, the only real need for upper body strength is to hold on. The rest is overkill."

As an expert on cycling but not a biologist, Balkin is only speaking from experience, but science tends to agree for more empirical reasons. According to the *New York Times*, women tend to require less protein consumption to exert equal amounts of force, and estrogen is believed to be the magic ingredient that fuels this. Researchers at McMaster University in Canada found that men who ingested estrogen before cycling "burned more fat and a smaller percentage of protein or carbohydrates to fuel their exertions, just as women do." (They also grew lovely breasts and lost their sex drive. Kidding.) A separate study found that when biking similar distances, women seemed to do significantly less muscle damage to their systems.

But the most important factor: only a woman can pull off the right biking outfit. "It is no surprise that women appear far more comfortable wearing Lycra than men," Balkin argues. "The best a Lycra-clad guy can look in public is strange, while most look ridiculous, some freaky. No guy wearing tights and in his right mind walks into a local tavern after a ride unless accompanied by a small army of similarly-dressed compatriots."

Whatever the reason, it's more than just a fable of the tortoise and the hare. In real life, females as tortoises may not only be smarter runners (and bikers), but their shells also appear to give them the physical advantage of keeping their muscles intact in exercises that would decimate the hare.

CHAPTER 23

Women Live Longer

*God gave us all a penis and a brain but
only enough blood to run one at a time.*

—ROBIN WILLIAMS

Most people are dimly aware that, in the great longevity contest of life, women usually win. Culturally, the figure of the widow looms larger than the figure of the widower because that's how it is statistically: women outlive men.

Some suspect that modern medicine is an equalizer that may change that. After all, when it comes to quality and length of life, your general practitioner has become as important as your genes. True—but false. Courtesy of modern medicine, the average life span has certainly gotten longer for men. But the same has happened for women. Since women were already ahead, there they've stayed, maintaining a significant edge over men when it comes to, well, living.

Most studies rate that edge in the neighborhood of five years. (*The CIA World Factbook*, for instance, says that American women tend to live about 81 years, while American men merely live 75.5). Of those 85 and older in the United States, there are only 50 men per 100 women.

Many theories have tried to explain the disparity but most point to the female body's ability to keep its heart out of trouble. "One important reason," said Tom Perls, founder of the New England Centenarian study at Boston University, to *Time* magazine, "is the big delay—and advantage—women have over men in terms of cardiovascular disease, like heart attack and stroke. Women develop these problems usually in their 70s and 80s, about 20 years later than men, who develop them in their 50s and 60s."

But why?

Some attribute it, paradoxically, to the female tendency toward iron deficiency. Though iron deficiency weakens the body in some ways, the absence of iron also protects it from heart attack and stroke.

But there are other possible explanations too. Men tend to cope with stress far worse than women. They smoke more and eat more noxious fats and cholesterols. Then, of course, there is the issue of testosterone overload. Men tend to be a lot more cavalier about taking dumb risks than women—some of which are fatal.

There's even an evolutionary theory for this gap in life expectancy: In 2006, researchers at the University of Michigan attempted to explain why, even in nonhuman species such as chimpanzees, females still tend to outlive males. Their findings indicated that the biological imperative to attract mates is responsible for riskier behavior, and as they evolved to compete with other men, they paid a price in the form of weaker immune systems and less ability to digest the fat they consume.

In the end, women may simply be better biologically equipped for their twilight than men. Quick review: Men have both an X and a Y chromosome, whereas women have two Xs. As men age and their biological architecture starts to corrode, they continue to need both X and Y chromosomes. Women, however, need only one kind of chromosome—the X—to express their genes. This lets them accommodate the genetic breakdowns of age much better than men. Think of it in terms of engines. Men use a complex, two-part engine to power their bodies. If either one of those parts fails, everything is endangered. Women, on the other hand, use two simple, partially interchangeable engines. If one engine fails or is damaged, they can rely on the other.

In the end, the numbers speak for themselves. Girls don't just have more fun than guys. They have it *for longer*.

CHAPTER 24

Women Are Less Likely to Be Struck by Lightning

The reason lightning doesn't strike twice in the same place is that the same place isn't there the second time.

When it comes to long shots, unlikely mishaps, or chances of contracting rare diseases, it seems there is always one barometer: the chance of being struck by lightning. It's not about the *actual* odds; it's about comparing these events to that bolt from Zeus. Whether it's the odds of winning the lottery, getting bitten by a shark, or developing Capgras syndrome, it seems the matter always comes back to whether you are more likely to be struck by lightning and, often, the answer is yes. But despite all the talk about the chances of being hit by lightning, it seems all these prognostications miss one very relevant factor: whether you are a man or a woman.

It's hard to believe, but PopSci.com reports that from 1995 to 2008, a whopping 82 percent of those struck by lightning in the US were men. So what is it about men that makes them such attractive targets for the effects of an electrical storm? Their height? The experts don't seem to view that as significant. I'm sure many guys would tell you that they have a "magnetic" pull that could explain it. Whatever. That's obviously not it either—although that sort of hubris and bravado may be part of the explanation.

According to John Jensenius, a lightning expert from the National Weather Service, it's far simpler than that. "Men take more risks in lightning storms," he told PopSci.com. Men, Jensenius argues, just don't bother to seek shelter in a storm as often as women. Picture the bishop in *Caddyshack* playing golf with Bill Murray during a massive electrical storm. He defends his refusal to quit, saying: "The good Lord would never disrupt the best game of my life." Of course he is then struck by lightning as he misses the final shot.

In fact, almost half of all lightning-related deaths are connected to recreational or sports activities. A behavioral psychologist also quoted by PopSci.com attributes it to something about men being wired to attract females with bold behavior and the desire to attract mates by showing little fear. Maybe, but I'm guessing a man's "wiring" and "magnetism" are less the issue than sometimes guys just being dim bulbs.

Oh, and in case you were wondering about Capgras syndrome mentioned above, it's a rare disorder where the victim comes to mistakenly believe his/her significant other is an imposter. In severe cases, the victim attacks a relative or boyfriend/girlfriend in question. No studies yet on whether this is more of a male or female disease, but I think it's safe to say that the chances of being struck by lightning are better than that of contracting this "disease"—at least for men.

CHAPTER 25

Women Are Better Sleepers

Men who are unhappy, like men who sleep badly, are always proud of the fact.

—BERTRAND RUSSELL

Paramount among the nebulous and arbitrary responsibilities that come with the title "housewife" seems to be getting the family up and functioning in the morning—the kids to school, the dog fed, and the husband (lunch box in tow?) off to work. As the saying goes, "Mothers are those wonderful people who can get up in the morning before the smell of coffee." Sometimes working mothers even manage to pull a good night's sleep out of their multiple hats, leading many groggy-eyed boys to wonder what the secret is to getting a good chunk of beauty sleep and still being able to see the dawn. And they're humble about it too. It's not intentional—women just don't realize how much better their sleep is.

Women, especially older women, may complain more about their "lack" of sleep in the morning, but their bodies tend to do much better than men in getting the most out of their slumber. Men, on the other hand, tend to think they're getting more out of their sleep cycles than they actually are. In other words, Sleeping Beauty may have gotten far more out of her cursed slumber than Rip Van Winkle got out of his two-decade siesta, but Rip would have reflected more positively on the experience.

The results come from a study conducted by a group of Dutch researchers in late 2009 to evaluate differences in sleep quality between men and women. They gathered nearly a thousand subjects, watched their sleep cycles, and then looked for differences in how the men and women rated their sleeping experiences. It was very sci-fi: For six nights in a row, subjects were plugged into all sorts of tracking devices, including an "actigraph" that measured tossing and turning, and were observed for sleep interruptions throughout the night. They also kept a "sleep diary" in which they chronicled how many hours of sleep they thought they were getting and how long it took them to fall asleep.

The sleep diaries of both, it turns out, were inaccurate. However, according to Dutch scientist Henning Tiemeier, quoted in ScienceDaily.com, "Men completely, and much more than women, overestimate the quality of their sleep." Men slept more than half an hour less than they thought they did; women, about fifteen minutes more. The average both sexes reported, about seven hours, was the actual amount of time the women slept—the men slept a bit less than that. Men also woke up more often during the night and tossed and turned, diminishing the quality of their rest. Despite this, the researchers report, women are more likely to complain of insomnia and sleepless nights.

One potential factor is the difference in statistics on snoring. According to a Wisconsin Sleep Cohort study (as explained in

Scientific American), 44 percent of men snore, while only 28 percent of women do. Research from the British Sleep Foundation supports this finding. It found that 40 percent of all middle-aged people snore, but men tend to snore about 10 percent more often than women. This also means it's overwhelmingly men who are putting their health at risk (snoring is a symptom and sometimes the cause of various respiratory disorders).

Then there's the issue of drinking, which also seems to have a significant impact on the quality of sleep. Frank Sinatra once passed on the gem of wisdom that when people who don't drink wake up, "that's as good as they're going to feel all day." The Dutch research team studying gender and sleep also found that men were drinking twice as much as women, leading them to conclude that alcohol consumption was significantly hindering men's sleep quality, accounting for "some, but not all" of the difference in their sleep quality.

In a certain sense, the fact that men are so woefully inaccurate at estimating their sleep time might actually be a plus—ignorance, after all, is bliss, especially if it means you're functioning as if you had an extra half hour of sleep every night. Of course, the reality is that men are drinking and snoring themselves into restless nights while, miraculously, women are sleeping better even though they are far more likely to have a drunk, snorting noise machine next to them in the bed.

CHAPTER 26

Women Have Stronger Immune Systems

*If I knew I was going to live
this long, I'd have taken
better care of myself.*

—MICKEY MANTLE

For those men reading this book and feeling down or underappreciated, well, thank your lucky stars that you are not a bee. That's right, living an existence exclusively dedicated to reproduction, the drone (male) suffers innumerable injustices at the hands of the queen. Drones have no say in what goes on with the most important of bee business matters—food production and nectar gathering. Having no stinger, they are also useless in protecting the hive, although sometimes the females will feed the male ego (sound familiar?) by permitting it to hover around uselessly and pretend it's about to attack an intruder. The only real bee business they are allowed to participate in is flimsily batting their wings in an attempt to generate heat when the hive gets too cold. Their main purpose, of course, is for mating, which guts out their reproductive organs and leads them to die. Nice.

In addition to the obvious inequalities in the life of a drone, his life span is also significantly shorter than that of the queen, even if he never commits the suicidal act of mating: forty to fifty days compared to the queen's two to five years—about 5 percent of the queen's life span.

The disparity between male and female life spans among humans is, of course, significantly less dramatic, but real (see Chapter 23). The largest gap between genders occurs in Russia, where, the *St. Petersburg Times* reports, women on average make it to seventy-one, while the average man doesn't make it to sixty. There are many explanations, related to accidents, behavior, diet, even lightning strikes (see Chapter 24), etc., but it also appears to be a biological advantage that keeps women healthier.

Scientists at McGill University confirmed what many suspected: women have stronger immune systems and are more resilient in the face of serious illnesses. (One of the few exceptions: the common cold, which women contract about nine times a year on average, compared to men's seven—but men whine about it more; see Chapter 2.)

So what's she got that I ain't got? It seems that estrogen is a warrior armed with a "secret ingredient" that fights off a dangerous enzyme that can stop the body from fighting disease. According to a 2009 BBC report, when injected with the disease-inducing enzyme caspase-12, male mice became more susceptible to disease, while females did not. Researchers believe the same applies to humans.

In that same BBC report, University of Cambridge researcher Dr. Leslie Knapp explained that "it only takes one male to reproduce with lots of females, but females are much more important in terms of producing offspring"—same as in the bee colony. Bottom line: the men are expendable!

The results of this for guys are staggering. In 2006, Dr. Marianne Legato, a specialist in male health (Why is there no word for this? Why is there gynecology but not andrology?), wrote an editorial in the *New York Times* detailing the obstacle course of illnesses a man must avoid to not die early in life. In fact, Dr. Legato persuaded national medical associations to stop devoting twice as much time taking care of women:

> Twice as many men as women die of coronary artery disease, which manifests itself a decade earlier in men than women; when it comes to cancer, the news for men is almost as bad. Women also have more vigorous immune systems than men: of the 10 most common infections, men are more likely to have serious encounters with seven of them.

To equalize the playing field, some researchers have even discussed treating men with estrogen as an immunological reinforcement, if the men are willing to live with the biological (and, umm, social) side effects. If scientists are right about the reasons behind women's resilience against disease, maybe nature would be kinder to men if they did more than flap their wings to try to heat up the hive.

CHAPTER 27

Women Are Getting Better Looking Faster Than Men

Sure God created man before woman.
But then you always make a rough
draft before the final masterpiece.

—AUTHOR UNKNOWN

Women are a lot prettier than men. With a touch of condescension, men love to gloat publicly about how much better looking their girl-friends, wives, or even daughters are than are they. "Thank goodness he/she looks more like my wife" is a common refrain. Still, if the women are more beautiful cliché isn't breaking news . . . how about this? Not only are women more attractive than men right now, they are going to *keep on getting more so*, achieving a fresh apex of attractiveness with every generation.

Not so for guys. Effectively, a genetic curse has been placed on them. It seems women are genetic go-getters who tend to give their children even better genes than they themselves had. Whereas men, genetic slackers, are going to stay more or less the same—and therefore, relatively speaking, are going to keep on getting uglier. Ouch.

According to a study of two thousand American men and women conducted by Markus Jokela at the University of Helsinki (and reported by the UK's *Times*), attractive women procreate 16 percent more than other women. Now couple that with a study from the London School of Economics of 2,972 men and women that found 56 percent of couples featuring at least one "beautiful" person had female children.

Call it Darwinism as retouched by Anna Wintour. Attractive women are having more children; and a majority of offspring of attractive people, male and female alike, are female.

Brace for a major demographic shift as men are being bred into comparative hideousness. The passing of every generation is going to add to the disproportion that already exists between the number of good-looking women and good-looking men.

It's tough to say who should be declaring victory over the fact that attractive women are well en route, demographically, to overrunning the men: the humdrum-looking men—a modest percentage of whom will be chosen, by reluctant default, to pair off with the increasingly beautiful women—or the female genetic victors.

CHAPTER 28

Women Have a Better Sense of Smell

If men have a smell it's usually an accident.

—ACTOR/COMEDIAN JEFF FOXWORTHY

Stinky locker rooms, unkempt bachelor pads, the remnant odor of old cigarettes and stale alcohol in a backroom casino or frat house—men get a bad rap when it comes to their scent. It's especially pronounced compared to the rosy, lineny, fresh smell often attributed to ladies. Part of this is probably the chorus of women themselves complaining about their guys' dirty, smelly socks. Now another possible explanation has appeared that extends beyond just suggesting that the ladies are nitpicky: it turns out women actually have a more finely tuned sense of smell than men that makes them acutely aware of that old kimchi in the fridge.

For the same reason that women are better at identifying complex flavors in beer (see Chapter 3), they are also more adept at recognizing smells at large, especially on their sometimes stinky male counterparts. This might be why they're more prone to breaking out the Febreze and spending an inordinate amount of time at a fine toiletries store, and may even explain why they seem to appreciate things like flowers more than men do.

Several studies in the late nineteenth century (conducted by men, of course) initially concluded that the opposite was true, but as technology developed with which to better measure the senses, the evidence grew increasingly conclusive that women were better equipped to pick up and recognize smells, and that it was far more difficult to disguise scents from women than men. A 2002 American study from the BBC showed that women were able to identify smells at much lower concentrations than men, and that even experience did not help the men. Professor Tim Jacob at Cardiff University told the BBC that the reason for this seems to be hormonal, since "the structure of the nose is the same in women as men. They don't have any more receptors in the nose."

Later studies support that conclusion, including an April 2009 one on identifying sweat, from the Monell Chemical Senses Center in Philadelphia. Why study smelly sweat? Well, what else should a Chemical Senses Center study? No, seriously, scientists have found that smells carry key biological information, such as the strength of a man's genes or when a woman is at her most fertile, so it makes sense that a woman's nose is even more finely tuned to identify male smells than female ones. "It is quite difficult to block a woman's awareness of body odor. In contrast, it seems rather easy to do so in men," said neuroscientist Charles Wysocki, who conducted the study (as reported in the online magazine *LiveScience*).

Using a smell of sweat that was measured equally potent to the noses of both men and women, the Chemical Senses Center masked it with a variety of thirty-two fragrances, one by one. Of those thirty-two, men were unable to recognize the sweat through nineteen of them. The women were only fooled by two of them.

So yes, a majority of women can tell a guy is sweaty through that cheap cologne. It's probably best to save the money and just shower more often or invest in some of the good stuff. Oh, and throw out the trash; no amount of Lysol is going to fix that.

PART V

WOMEN ARE BETTER PROFES-SIONALS

CHAPTER 29

Women Are Better Cops

Marge, you being a cop makes you The Man! Which makes me the woman— and I have no interest in that, besides occasionally wearing the underwear, which as we discussed is strictly a comfort thing.

—HOMER SIMPSON

Colorful toy guns, shiny fake badges, and plastic handcuffs aren't usually at the top of any little girl's wish list. And when so many of pop culture's top cops are beacons of masculinity—whether they be rugged Kojak types or the slick (and now dated) heroes of *Miami Vice*—can you really blame them? Girls didn't even have a Police Officer Barbie to look up to until 1993. The vibrant machismo of the law enforcement mystique only gets more pronounced from there, with women often seen as too small, too emotional, or too vulnerable to handle the pressures of catching criminals for a living.

Well, recent studies are proving that the world would benefit from more little girls being given police toy sets as birthday gifts. Women are proving to be, on the whole, both more trustworthy and less corruptible than their male counterparts in law enforcement. And, maybe even more surprisingly, they're beating men at one of the toughest and arguably most important parts of the job: defusing a violent situation. Governments around the world are taking notice.

Lima, Peru, is a place the US Department of State warns is teeming with "violent crime, including carjacking, assault, sexual assault, and armed robbery." It also has a decades-long corruption problem in its police force, trickling down from the highest-ranked law enforcement officers to the lowest-ranked meter maids. A half a world away, Russian law enforcement authorities in the city of Volgograd faced their own corruption problem. According to the Russian Interior Ministry, crime within the police force rose 46.8 percent nationally between 2004 and 2005 and spanned every area of law enforcement, from passports to criminal investigations to, yes, traffic cops. Both the governments of Lima and Volgograd had a serious police integrity problem, and both governments came up with the same solution: hire more women.

In Lima, officers were convinced to make the move by a combination of polls showing a plurality of Peruvians believed women were more trustworthy than men, as well as studies showing corruption levels among female workers to be lower. In Volgograd, public opinion skewed in the same direction. Slowly but surely, the twenty-first century saw an increase in female traffic cops until, by 2009, the entire force of traffic cops on the streets of Lima was female. In Volgograd, the police chief created an all-female street force in 2006.

They had good reason to believe that the inclination toward honesty among female politicians (see Chapter 18) would also appear in their law enforcement counterparts. What they perhaps didn't expect was that women don't just outperform their male counterparts in judiciously distributing traffic fines—they're better officers at the highest and most dangerous levels of the job.

In the 2004 study *Gender Differences in Leniency Towards Police*, professors at the University of Maribor in Slovenia found that female police officers consider moral transgressions more serious than their male counterparts do and are less tolerant of corruption within their ranks than are men. Asked to evaluate a number of scenarios in which officers were behaving immorally, women were significantly more inclined to report police brutality: "Of all groups, female police officers were the least tolerant of this kind of behavior, as shown by their willingness to report it." They were also less trusting of the integrity of police officers:

> Police brutality and a preferential treatment of police offenders are more acceptable in the male mentality.
>
> Also, male participants had a somewhat higher level of trust in police officers' moral standards than did female participants, as shown by three individual cases and a composite measure of beliefs about other officers' perception of the seriousness of corruption.

The fact that female police officers hold themselves and their male counterparts to a higher standard may have something to do with the fact that they can deal with the added pressure. Research shows that in situations involving violent crime and the potential for excessive force—the most dangerous scenarios for an officer—

female cops are more likely to get the job done without overstepping their authority.

A study by the National Center for Women & Policing examined Los Angeles police brutality statistics between 1990 and 1999. Male officers, it turns out, were disproportionately accountable for excessive-force lawsuits. Of the $66.3 million Los Angeles had to pay in judgments for out-of-court police brutality settlements, 95.8 percent was on account of men behaving badly. And male police officers aren't just more likely to jump the gun on use of force; when they do it, it's more expensive. The payout ratios for victims of male police killings to that by females is 43:1; for assault and battery, it's 32:1. The study concludes:

> Women police officers are less authoritarian and rely less on physical force and more on verbal skills in handling altercations than their male counterparts. As a result, women police officers are better at defusing potentially violent confrontations with citizens and are less likely to become involved in problems with excessive force than male police officers.

In other words, women are less prone to breaking the rules, less expensive when they *do*, and they have a much lower tolerance for bad behavior in others. But there is a downside: with a female force, you're probably going to have a tougher time BS-ing your way out of paying for that parking ticket.

CHAPTER 30

Women Are Better World Leaders

In January 1960, a reporter for the London Standard *approached Winston Churchill at a reception. "Sir Winston, what is your comment on the prediction made the other day that in the year 2000, women will rule the world?" "They still will, will they?" Churchill grunted.*

"If only women ruled the world" is often said as a dreamy, utopian, lofty, but totally unrealistic goal. Well, according to a recent poll conducted by the Pew Research Center, women do run the world and run it well, and everyone is just thrilled they're running it, frankly. OK, that's not actually what the poll says. But in a 2008 survey, 2,250 adult respondents ranked men or women as superior in eight different categories of political aptitude deemed "very important or absolutely essential" to leadership. The categories were themselves ranked from most important (honesty) to least important (creativity).

The results were, to put it plainly, blindingly one-sided. In seven out of the eight categories, the respondents described women as either better than or, in the cases of working harder and ambition, the equals of men. And these weren't thin majorities either: in each of the five categories in which they were judged superior, the women vaulted over the men by a minimum margin of 24 percent.

The details: an astounding 30 percent more respondents (50 percent to 20 percent) thought women possessed greater honesty—the most important attribute for politics, according to the PRC's survey of the populace—than men. Another result, easy enough to predict, remained notable for its lopsidedness: 80 percent of respondents thought women more compassionate than men, compared with a meager 5 percent who thought men the more compassionate sex.

Only in terms of decisiveness, the fourth most relevant category of political aptitude, according to the study, did a greater percentile of respondents (44 percent) deem men superior to women (33 percent).

If this poll is any guide, women should be running the world—or at least its democratic parts—right now. Clearly, in a realm where public perception is everything, the public's gigantically favorable perception of "female traits" in potential leaders isn't trivial and, in any given election, a female candidate should enjoy a hefty edge over a male one.

So then wait. Why *aren't* women running the world today?

Female politicians still struggle hard, of course, with a residue of the old sexism—the old reluctance to defer to the missus. Despite the fact that most believe women have just what it takes for public office, only a frail minority of that same public—6 percent!— think women, overall, make better political leaders. Hmm.

How long can the public keep up this intellectual inconsistency? Manifoldly better equipped for political office, according to the public, women are destined to get a mandate from that public. If you were a betting man—or rather, if you were a man striving to bet as well as a woman (see Chapter 9)—you'd do well to focus less on the Johns and Steves of the ballot box and direct your attention to its Janes and Susans. The signs are up and the results are in: women are poised to rout men in the politics of the future.

CHAPTER 31

Women Are Better Hedge Fund Managers

*As a woman, I find it very
embarrassing to be in a meeting
and realize I'm the only one
in the room with balls.*

—RITA MAE BROWN, *STARTING FROM SCRATCH:
A DIFFERENT KIND OF WRITERS' MANUAL*

We tend to think of Wall Street as about as hospitable to women as a Wild West saloon. Which is to say, not. You need ego, testosterone, and a passionate fondness for certain of our language's more flexible four-letter words. That strictly-business savagery is supposedly essential to success in finance and maybe even more so with hedge fund managers, who are often betting on the failure of companies. It's also what women characteristically lack. Right?

That's what you hear.

Turns out we were misinformed.

For the past decade, women have outperformed men at one of the most glamorous latitudes of the financial world: hedge funds. Yes, hedge funds. During the boom, or bubble, hedge funds became the envy of just about every industry for the sheer numbers they delivered to those on the "inside." When the recession struck, hedge funds shriveled at a spectacular rate. What goes up must come down. Except unlike physical gravity, financial gravity appears to work differently for men and women. During the boom, women hedge fund managers did the best; during the bust, they suffered the least—they bucked the bronco better.

According to data tabulated by Hedge Fund Research (as reported in *Institutional Investor*):

[F]rom January 2000 through May 31, 2009 . . . women who ran hedge funds delivered nearly double the investment performance of their male counterparts. Female managers produced average annualized returns of 9 percent, versus 5.82 percent for the men.

Most impressive in an era when profits proved spectral and abstract losses real and devastating, female hedge fund managers lost dramatically less during the downturn. *BusinessWeek* observed of the same data: "When financial markets were cratering, funds run by women lost 9.6%, compared with a 19% decline for men."

How to explain this? In a period that punished risk-taking, were women just reaping the benefits of an inborn timidity, an innate aversion to risk? Or was something more complex at work? *Institutional Investor* quoted Judi McLean Parks, a business professor at Washington University in St. Louis: "It's not that women are averse to risk. It's just that they are less likely to take the *big* risk."

So it's not that women are shackled by caution; they just don't get suckered by visions of grandeur. Generally speaking, women prefer a probable double to striking out swinging for the stands. The same cannot be said for men.

Jacquelyn Zehner, the first female trader to make partner at Goldman Sachs, was quoted in *Institutional Investor* in November 2009: "I firmly believe if we had more women in financial management, we might not have experienced such a severe financial crisis."

And yet as discussed in Chapter 12, women are still only managing 3 percent of the money currently in play in global hedge funds.

The superiority of female hedge fund managers may herald a sea change in Wall Street demographics, for good reason. Clearly, women have been doing something right, and men have been doing it, at the least, less right. In particular, if the times are turbulent and you need someone to fatten or just protect a large portfolio, your best bet will be a Ms. or Mrs.

CHAPTER 32

Women Are
Better Doctors

*A male gynecologist is like an auto
mechanic who has never owned a car.*

—CARRIE SNOW, COMEDIAN

Ever find yourself scouring for a doctor covered by your insurance? You know the type of physician you need and the most convenient location, but the names, well, they become a daunting sea of anonymity, about as instructive as reading a phone book. The As through Ds have a distinct advantage because you have not completely lost interest yet. If you do make it down that far, maybe you even show a bias toward, let's say, Dr. Kelly Walsh, because you think, maybe just maybe, she is Kate Walsh's mother, and Kate plays a great doctor on *Grey's Anatomy* and *Private Practice* (Dr. Addison Montgomery). Something, anything to help guide you to a good doctor.

Well, in addition to looking at the hospital she or he works for and asking friends for suggestions, there is another more objective factor to consider. All other things being equal, there is a good case to be made that you should go for the Amys, Jennifers, or Felicias.

In 2009, the British government reported the results of its largest study ever of medical performance. They compiled a database of information on all the doctors and dentists investigated for medical misconduct or incompetence over a period of eight years. All of them. In that time, just 20 percent of the doctors referred for a more thorough investigation were women.

OK—but wait. How many of the doctors in England were women at that time? How about double that number? Forty percent of the working doctors and dentists were female and yet almost 80 percent of the medical miscreants, four in five, were male. 3,635 men compared to 873 female troubled practitioners.

Most (two-thirds) of the total pool were reported for their less than professional clinical skills, but about a quarter were referrals for health reasons such as depression and addiction. Top that off with the ones investigated for inappropriate behavior and you have a disproportionately male problem.

Among the worst offenders—the ones actually barred from resuming work—the numbers were even worse for the guys. Two hundred ninety male hospital workers were kicked out compared to fifty women. Among general practitioners, two hundred men got the boot compared to just twenty-nine women.

Incidentally, they started monitoring this, in part, because of a guy who dubbed himself the "fastest gynecologist in the west." Ugh. You can see how this ends. Let's just say he was involved in a series of bungled operations and lost his medical license.

In the US, the numbers appear to be equally lopsided. A 2010 report from the American Medical Association found that male physicians were twice as likely to be sued as female ones—47.5 to 23.9 percent. There are a host of possible explanations, including riskier specialties that include more male doctors, but maybe it's far simpler: maybe, just maybe, as a group, female doctors are more careful. Dr. Pauline Chen wrote in the *New York Times*:

> Several studies have shown that female doctors tend to be more encouraging and reassuring, use shared decision-making, ask more psychosocial questions and spend more time—up to 10 percent more—with patients than male doctors do.

Picking a doctor can be an intimidating and life-changing decision, so making that choice based on something as superficial as the gender of the doctor is not a particularly smart strategy. But if that's all you have, why not play the odds?

CHAPTER 33

Women Are Better Newscasters

I can not imagine that a woman can read the news without breaking out into tears.

—POPULAR GERMAN NEWSCASTER KARL-HEINZ KOPCKE

If you are forty-plus, you will recall the days of all-male local news-casts: two guys sitting at an anchor desk along with a jock-y male sportscaster and the always obligatory kooky weatherman. After the harder news segments were over, the men would often sit around and bond over frat-boyish jokes (usually at the expense of the weather guy). On the national level, all of the leading news anchors were male too: Walter (Cronkite), John (Chancellor), David (Brinkley), etc. Then along came a pioneering woman named Barbara (Walters), who shook up the boys club by refusing to settle for what she called a "tea pourer" job doing lighter news on the *Today* show. She became the first woman to coanchor a national evening news program in 1976 (the *ABC Evening News*), leading what became a sea change at anchor desks.

In fact, just thirty years ago, only 13 percent of US reporters were women. Now, more than half of all US reporters and anchors are women. In Switzerland, 64 percent of newscasters are female. It's 66 percent in Austria, and in Germany, where Karl-Heinz Kopcke of the choice quote above worked, it's now a whopping 84 percent female. These days, can you even imagine an all-male anchor team? It's not just hard to imagine because female viewers might feel excluded—it also just looks, well, weird, and almost never happens anymore. A team of two women is considered far more acceptable than two guys. A *Salon* article calling 2008 "The Year of the Woman" singled out Katie Couric and Rachel Maddow in the newscasters category. Add to that list other high-profile women in news like Christiane Amanpour, Greta Van Susteren, Meredith Vieira, Ann Curry, Robin Roberts, and a host of others, and it's clear that it's only been getting better for women in the news ever since.

So what happened? How did we reach a point where a Katie and a Diane (Sawyer) made up the majority of the evening news anchors? Well, you could certainly argue that they just earned it with hard work. There is no question that they have become the sort of "brands" that any network is seeking. But there also may be something else at play: credibility. A significant study shows that when a woman newscaster reads a report, that report is viewed as more credible than if it comes from a man. The 2008 study from Switzerland took account of just about every possible variable to ensure its integrity and accuracy. Researchers gathered 160 subjects and had them sit and watch real newscasts, then fill out questionnaires about the credibility of the newscasters based on gender (and age). The findings? "Messages read by female newscasters were evaluated as being more credible."

While the rigorous research into gender and news is relatively new because female newscasters didn't become part of the norm until recently, there was a study from as far back as 1978 that showed "males were perceived as being less verbal, qualified, and thus less credible than females." In a world where credibility is the coin of the realm, you would think that would make women the obvious choice across the board.

But, as with so many things, there's a catch. The same Swiss study that proved the message or report read by a woman was deemed more credible also showed that male newscasters were still considered "more credible" overall. This quote from the study would be hilarious if it didn't so clearly reflect reality: "Men were considered to be more credible but the messages they read were perceived as being less credible." People thought they trusted the men more, but when the actual report was read, the women came out on top. This echoes a similar attitude toward female politicians (see Chapter 18), where women have more of the qualities voters are seeking in a candidate and yet far more men are still elected.

Bottom line: male newscasters seem to be running on the fumes of credibility from days past. You would think that if women present reports that are considered more credible, not far into the future they will win the all-around credibility war as well. But then again, past studies have found that a news report is more credible if "read loudly with a deep voice." So who the heck knows?

CHAPTER 34

Women Are Better Loan Officers

I looked the man in the eye.
I was able to get a sense of his soul.
I knew that President Putin was a
man with whom I could work.

—GEORGE W. BUSH

How often have we heard, in movies or from friends, men claiming to have recognized fellow men as authentic, trustworthy, the genuine article—men vouching for other men on the basis of a "gut feeling," a look in the eye, or a handshake? Far too often, it turns out. Statistics suggest that women possess a much sharper intuition than do men—not just in emotional and romantic matters, as is often discussed, but also in business.

Think about it: What job by its description alone requires the most adept ability to judge superficially and substantively whether you want to do business with a person? Sure, human-resources professionals probably do it every day. They interview prospective candidates and at least help make the decision about whether to hire the person, but there is no truly objective way to judge that success.

The one job where this type of judgment is paramount and can be objectively assessed? A person whose sole mission is to figure out whom you can trust to make good on a promise? A loan officer. (After all, loan-sharking is illegal, and they don't keep great records of the number of legs broken.)

The most definitive study to date comes from banks in, of all places, Albania. They kept detailed records on the gender of the loan officer in 43,000 loan applications, 31,000 of which were granted from January 1996 to December 2006.

The loans were mainly for business and housing improvement, so the goal was clearly making money, not philanthropy. The question: who did a better job of figuring out which first-time loans were the right ones to make? Yes, female loan officers had fewer problem loans both with male and female borrowers. Furthermore, loans by female borrowers and borrowers screened and monitored by female loan officers were least likely to turn problematic.

So why were the women better? Well, we know what it wasn't. The rigorous study ensured the women did not get the less risky borrowers. Nor were the female loan officers more restrictive in the screening process or more experienced. In fact, the female loan officers were, on average, roughly two years younger than their male counterparts. And no, the female loan officers did not have a lighter workload than their male colleagues.

The study speculated that maybe they had fewer other job options so they had to be more careful, or maybe they were less mobile, or just more risk averse. One thing is for certain—the women loan officers were just, well, better. Loan sharks take note: Work with women and you may be able to save some serious cash on "enforcement costs."

CHAPTER 35

Women Are Better at Navigating a Tough Economy

It is now possible for a flight attendant to get a pilot pregnant.

—RICHARD J. FERRIS, PRESIDENT OF UNITED AIRLINES

In the 1980 classic *Nine to Five*, three office gals (played by Dolly Parton, Lily Tomlin, and Jane Fonda) kidnap their obnoxiously crude, sexist male boss after his loyal assistant overhears of their fantasies of murdering him. After a series of larger-than-life follies and misunderstandings, and more than a few changes in the office while the boss is "away," they succeed in getting the boss a "promotion" far, far away—and are left to run the company and help it prosper.

In the real world, the female professional collaborative has not quite kidnapped all its male counterparts and sent them to Brazil just yet, but it's starting to look more and more like that might not even be necessary. Men, it seems, just aren't able to navigate a tough economy the way women can.

The statistics for men from this most recent recession aren't great: they suffered a steeper unemployment drop and left 35 percent of American women (and growing) responsible for at least half of their household income. Traditionally masculine industries—construction, assembly lines, rural blue-collar work, banking—were hit hard (which, for those of you counting, could leave almost half the Village People looking for a new costume). But the story of the recession isn't primarily a story of the failure of men: it's a story of the success of women.

Not only are the traditionally female-dominated industries the ones expected to grow the fastest in the near future, but women are making inroads in historically male-dominated careers as well. This as their male counterparts are having more trouble switching gears, finding jobs, and, as discussed in Chapter 15, succeeding in school.

The July 2010 cover story in the *Atlantic* dramatically titled "The End of Men" cited statistics that women held 26 percent more white-collar jobs than they did thirty years ago and were slated to overtake men in the number of managerial (but not yet top-level) jobs in the very near future.

Among the professions where the presence of women has increased most significantly are medicine (see Chapter 32), banking (see Chapter 34), and the law. And while women make inroads in traditionally male fields, guys have yet to crack the glass ceiling in careers like nursing and teaching. In fact, men made up fewer than 10 percent of teaching assistants, as well as preschool and kindergarten teachers, in 2009. Moreover, according to the Bureau of Labor Statistics, they constituted only 18 percent of elementary and middle schoolteachers, and at the high school level, fared only slightly better, making up 45 percent of faculty. As those industries grow while physical labor jobs shrink, the face of the "working man" in America is becoming increasingly feminine.

In September 2010, *Newsweek* reported that the future looks pretty bleak for men as well:

> Of the 15.3 million new jobs projected to sprout up over the next decade, the vast majority will come in fields that currently attract far more women than men. In fact, men dominate only two of the 12 job titles expected to grow the most between 2008 and 2018: construction worker and accountant. The rest, including teachers (501,000 new positions), registered nurses (582,000), home health aides (461,000), and customer-service reps (400,000), remain heavily female.

And talk about bringing home the bacon and frying it in a pan: as of March 2010, more than half of Americans who hold more than one job—3.7 million—are women. (See also Chapter 15, proving that women are better multitaskers.)

Maybe part of the problem is that guys have trouble controlling their emotions, and their tempers, when the going gets tough at the office. A 2010 survey from the *Harvard Business Review* found that "Male teenagers feel an astonishing amount of hostility in the work-place," with 60 percent of young male workers saying they would punch a coworker in the face if they could do it with impunity. Forty percent would punch their bosses. Yikes.

In this new world where physical strength is increasingly irrelevant, a larger percentage of men are going to be the ones raising the kids, cooking, and cleaning (and for that matter, the plot of *Nine to Five* may be enacted regularly for quality control purposes). You know *The Real Househusbands of New Jersey* is going to be huge!

CHAPTER 36

Women Are Better at Gathering Mushrooms in a Remote Part of Mexico

*I hate women because they always
know where things are.*

—VOLTAIRE

Forget all those stereotypes you heard from the Super Mario Bros. about women and mushrooms: a scientific study conducted by the National Autonomous University of Mexico has found conclusive evidence that women are much more efficient at tracking down as many mushrooms in the countryside as possible within a given time frame. Yes, it's true, and yes, it's real.

Wait. And this warranted its own chapter? OK, it's true that it didn't quite fit neatly into any of the others, but more important, this study alone serves as a microcosm that reflects so much of the evidence in this book: that women (in an area unaffected by so many other outside factors) were more efficient and effective, took fewer unnecessary risks, and achieved equal or better results.

The study, as reported in the *Economist*, sent two teams of villagers from the state of Tlaxcala, divided by gender, to gather mushrooms across the countryside for two wet seasons. Using GPS tracking, they were able to see exactly how far each of them traveled to find their far-flung fungi. In the end, both men and women collected the same amount of mushrooms, but the men walked much farther and spent 70 percent more energy doing so.

Why? According to the researchers, the guys went for the big swing, seeking out the thick troves of mushrooms, which often took them on long treks (think of the guy who needs to find the parking spot closest to the entrance to the mall even if it means driving in circles first), while the women were content with closer, sparser patches. The men also seemed to prefer trying to come up with complete mental maps and then locating themselves on them, while the women navigated the terrain by memorizing landmarks. The study's author says that this supports the notion that men's navigational sense is better suited to hunting: "Women perform better and more readily adopt search strategies appropriate to a gathering lifestyle."

OK, maybe. But there is a broader conclusion to come from this study that is significantly more applicable to the lives of those of us who don't happen to live in a remote village that sustains itself on mushrooms. The male choice to travel farther in search of larger patches means that, in reality, the men were out wasting time getting lost and trying to find their way back (without asking anyone for directions, of course—see Chapter 20).

Nor are those talents lost on urban females either. Take the following study conducted by researchers from the University of California at Santa Barbara and Yale, which asked forty-five men and forty-one women at a farmer's market to use a compass to identify where they had purchased certain produce such as strawberries or tomatoes.

"Men were making 33 degree pointing error, when women were around 25 degree, which is a 27 percent improvement," Max Krasnow, a member of the research team, told the *Daily Telegraph*. That's right—apparently you can't even trust a man to give accurate directions to the lettuce stand, never mind a location greater than a few yards from your starting point. And don't even think about asking where the most accessible local mushrooms are in rural Mexico.

In addition to demonstrating that researchers now have the time and advanced tools to track men and women foraging for mushrooms in the countryside and even in a local farmer's market, the results are reminiscent of why women are better hedge fund managers, drivers, cops, doctors, investors, loan officers, and gamblers, and maybe even why the guys get struck by lightning more often: The men took the big risks, many of them striking out (or in the case of lightning, getting struck), and at best ended up in the same place as their female counterparts while exhausting significantly more time and effort. Women, meanwhile, stayed on courses they already knew well rather than taking the risk of straying too far from the familiar, and they had the patience to weed through, in this case, sparser mushroom patches to get the most out of the landscape.

Many (mostly men) will argue that the mushroom study is

pointless, with no application to the life of the average American. Most of those men have probably never been in a situation where they've had to gather as many wild mushrooms as possible for a living. They have, however, probably made a life-or-death situation out of finding the remote control after the couch ate it or the dog hid it under the bed, and have looked on helplessly as the woman of the house found the missing object in no time. They will immediately get the point of this study.

CLOSING ARGUMENT

You have now seen the evidence: dozens of distinct areas where studies and research show that women are better or just cooler than men.

Do I believe that this conclusively determines that, for example, men take longer to get ready than women? No. I have put forth a study—evidence—that suggests a long-standing stereotype about men and women may be false. (And come on, if that one is true, the men are really in trouble.) But many other myths were far more definitively shattered in areas that have long been viewed as typically male, such as dealing with pain, gambling, endurance sports, driving, and even competitive eating.

There is no question that men still have certain biological advantages related to size and strength, but women have an equally powerful edge when it comes to health: living longer (whining less about pain) and smelling, tasting, and sleeping better as they evolve into more beautiful beings than their male counterparts.

As a guy, I like shooting from the hip and giving directions even if I'm not entirely certain they're accurate (and despite the study cited here, I don't know that I'm ready to concede that most women are better news-casters!). I enjoy classically guy endeavors like ensuring that my home stereo system has enough speakers so that the impact of the subwoofer can be heard clearly throughout my home. In fact, in many ways we guys still have it easier in our society. But that's just another argument in favor of women—the fact that they have overcome obstacles.

Most persuasive, however, are the consistent themes throughout this book that prove women make fewer errors and are less corruptible, more conscientious, and more effective with their time and risk-taking. Together this creates a compelling case for women. And only now are we seeing the effects of that superiority, from the workplace to the home to the remote mushroom fields of Mexico.

I think this is proof beyond a reasonable doubt that women, as a group, are the superior gender, but that verdict remains in your hands.

I rest my case.

ABOUT THE AUTHOR

Dan Abrams has been the chief legal analyst for *NBC News* and is the founder of the Abrams Media Network.

Dan was the general manager of MSNBC during which time ratings grew by 62 percent and he branded the network "The Place for Politics." Prior to his management appointment, Abrams hosted *The Abrams Report*, a nightly legal affairs program, and later *Verdict with Dan Abrams.*

In the past two years the Abrams Media Network has launched media news site Mediaite.com, fashion and style site Styleite.com, Geekosystem .com for tech lovers, and Sportsgrid.com. He is also the cofounder of Gossipcop.com, the first major website to police the gossip industry for inaccuracies in reporting.

Abrams, a Columbia University School of Law grad, is also a recognized writer. He has published articles in the *New York Times*, the *Wall Street Journal, Newsweek*, the *American Lawyer*, and the *Yale Law and Policy Review*, among many others. He has also written for online media such as the *Huffington Post*, the *Daily Beast*, and, of course, regularly for Mediaite. He is also the legal columnist for *Men's Health* magazine.

Dan has never been married, so despite his admiration for women, evidenced by this book, that does not mean he necessarily knows how to talk to them.